CHINESE FIRMS GOING GLOBAL

Can They Succeed?

CHINESE
FIRMS
GOING
GLOBAL

CAN THEY SUCCEED?

Joseph Healy

Judo Capital, Australia & University of Queensland, Australia

World Scientific

NEW JERSEY · LONDON · SINGAPORE · BEIJING · SHANGHAI · HONG KONG · TAIPEI · CHENNAI · TOKYO

Published by

World Scientific Publishing Co. Pte. Ltd.
5 Toh Tuck Link, Singapore 596224
USA office: 27 Warren Street, Suite 401-402, Hackensack, NJ 07601
UK office: 57 Shelton Street, Covent Garden, London WC2H 9HE

Library of Congress Cataloging-in-Publication Data
Names: Healy, Joseph C., author.
Title: Chinese firms going global : can they succeed? / Joseph Healy (Judo
    Capital, Australia & University of Queensland, Australia).
Description: New Jersey : World Scientific, [2018] | Includes bibliographical
    references and index.
Identifiers: LCCN 2017061609| ISBN 9789813235939 (hc : alk. paper) | ISBN
    9789813237124 (pbk : alk. paper)
Subjects: LCSH: International business enterprises--China. | Investments,
    Foreign--China. | China--Commerce. | China--Foreign economic relations.
Classification: LCC HD2910 .H43 2018 | DDC 338.8/8951--dc23
LC record available at https://lccn.loc.gov/2017061609

British Library Cataloguing-in-Publication Data
A catalogue record for this book is available from the British Library.

For any available supplementary material, please visit
http://www.worldscientific.com/worldscibooks/10.1142/10876#t=suppl

Desk Editors: Chandrima Maitra/ Lixi Dong

Typeset by Stallion Press
Email: enquiries@stallionpress.com

Printed in Singapore

Preface

There has arguably never been a more exciting and complex era in which to write about the globalisation of Chinese firms than now, as China increases its engagement with the world and prosecutes ambitious economic goals, as well as more cautious diplomatic and military strategies. For much of the last three decades, I have been captivated and inspired by the transformation that has been taking place in China and how Chinese business has adapted to globalisation. Much has been written about the economic and social impact of Inbound Foreign Direct Investment (IFDI) with the transfer-in of Western resources and expertise. Less has been written, in an accessible way at least, on the unleashing of the entrepreneurial spirit and Outbound Foreign Direct Investment (OFDI) as Chinese firms have gone global.

My vantage point is primarily that of a senior banker who regularly visits China while based in Australia since 2001, with its close dependency on China (but deep-rooted Anglo-Saxon culture) and secondly as an academic interested in Chinese history and culture, as well as its contemporary political, geopolitical, and economic history. My intellectual curiosity was fuelled by two courses of study: first an MSc in International Management in China at the School of Oriental and African Studies (SOAS), University of London, and then, while on sabbatical in 2014–2015, an MA in Contemporary Chinese Studies at the University of Nottingham, Ningbo, China (UNNC).

At UNNC, I immersed myself in the management challenges that Chinese firms face in becoming international, having observed these first-hand as a senior bank executive. Though Chinese firms are latecomers, the pace at which they have been internationalising their operations has been one of the standout features of the global economy since the turn of the 21st century. This book was inspired by my dissertation research question: *How Important is Management Education to China's Success in the Global Economy?* The emphasis in this book is not, however, on management education *per se*, but on the importance of the 'Four Cs' necessary to succeed in a global economy, where, I believe, Chinese firms are handicapped in many ways. I define the Four Cs below.

Like for so many others, my views on the world are shaped by education and experience. In my case, these are steeped in classical economics when it comes to issues regarding the management of the firm: how factors of production are employed to optimise, sustainably, the economic contribution of the firm to its stakeholders, primarily its shareholders and society. I am convinced, as will become evident in the book, that the laws of economics, just like the laws of medicine, transcend markets, cultures, and geographies and that what holds true in the Western world will eventually hold true in China when it comes to key economic outcomes. I hold this core belief even though I also believe that China is unique in many ways.

As Chinese firms have globalised, I have been intrigued as to how they would manage the liabilities and hazards of foreignness — the additional costs of being a stranger in a strange land. As I argue in this book, there is evidence that these costs are higher for Chinese firms than for other foreign firms. This may be due in part because of confirmation biases concerning China, which can result in a form of discrimination.

A range of factors such as history, culture, capabilities, and discrimination may in aggregate create what preeminent University of Cambridge Chinese scholar Peter Nolan has described as 'insurmountable challenges' for Chinese firms in the international economy. At a minimum, the nature of these challenges reinforces the importance of management capabilities and the role management education can play in developing those capabilities, but not necessarily management education as it is taught today.

I must declare a prejudice that holds true for Chinese firms as it does for firms in any market. First, when it comes to defining and measuring success in business, I believe that firms are successful only when they can create sustainable value for their owners by earning a return on invested capital (ROIC) that is at least equal to their risk-adjusted cost of capital (i.e. they are creating economic profits, not just simple accounting profits). Firms achieve this by having a competitive advantage, or firm-specific advantages (FSAs), that allow them to grow their revenues and achieve a satisfactory ROIC. Firms that fail to achieve an ROIC at least equal to their risk-adjusted cost of capital operate at a loss in an economic sense regardless of their reported accounting-based profits; such firms return less to the economy than they consume in resources, thus destroying wealth. Such destruction can lead to material macroeconomic consequences if it is wide scale and prolonged; they can take years to manifest, but manifest they will. For China, this is an important theory.

This book emphasises management capabilities.[1] I believe that most business failure occurs because of management failure (*businesses do not fail; it's management that fails*). The difference between a great, good, mediocre, and poor business is management. Thirty-plus years as a banker to businesses small and large and being a keen student of business have ingrained this belief into me deeply. Certainly, tough industry conditions can defeat the ablest of management; as Warren Buffet once said, 'When a management with a reputation for brilliance tackles a business with a reputation for bad economics, it is the reputation of the business that remains intact'. The enduring truth is, however, that businesses and economies transform and succeed because of excellent, often bold, leadership

---

[1] Throughout this book I use the terms *capabilities* and *competencies* interchangeably. Also, when it comes to authors of cited material mentioned in the text, I have attempted to always use a date in parentheses to enable readers to go directly to the bibliography. For ease of reference I also make extensive use of footnotes to highlight referenced material.

as well as highly skilful management that knows how to get things done: how to execute on strategy, not just develop strategy and communicate through impressive PowerPoints. Execution defines the gap between great and mediocre businesses and between great and mediocre managers. It was the leadership of Deng Xiaoping and others like Jiang Zemin, Zhu Rongji, Hu Yaobang, Zhao Ziyang, and Qian Qichen, for example, that began the rejuvenation of China. The so-called 'economic miracle' (which has seen close to 500 million people lifted from poverty — the greatest economic achievement in history) was created by the superior leadership of individuals rather than by any divine intervention normally associated with miracles. In business as in life, things generally do not happen without people making them happen. This is why I believe that the defining factor in business, political, and economic success is the quality of management and leadership.

Throughout this book, I place emphasis on the 'Four Cs' of sustained competitive advantage in international markets — *core capabilities* (firm-specific assets (FSAs) and 'administrative heritage' as Bartlett and Ghoshal (2002) emphasise), *cultural adaptability* (experienced and skilled in cross-cultural management), *competencies of management* (proven, multi-disciplined management capabilities; the essential human capital critical to success in international markets), and *country of origin* (modern history in global markets, international reputation, and country-specific assets (CSAs)). Using this framework, I assess how well equipped Chinese firms are to overcome hazards such as discrimination and succeed, particularly in developed markets. I explore the extent to which Chinese firms are weak in one or more of the Four Cs and suggest that a compensatory Fifth C — *cooperation with government* — might better explain their international strategy.

The reader will find many references to 'China and the West' in this book. One should keep in mind Edward Said's sage advice about the danger of overly simplistic binary classifications of 'East and West'. Said highlighted the principal dogmas in *Orientalism* (Said, 1978), in which, in contrast to the East, the West is viewed as rational, developed, and superior. When a former Australian Prime

Minister said 'Western civilisation provides our comparative advantage amongst the cultures of the world', he was falling into the dogmatic trap that Said warned against (Bryant, 2015: 238). It is my deeply held view that, in any discourse on China and Chinese firms, recognising and respecting the differences in history, culture, institutions, and political systems is critical if an intelligent assessment is to be made and relationships established and if economic activity is to flow. Strong social and cultural ties are the foundation for sustainable cross-border economic development. When it comes to China, there are no short-cuts. An intelligent analyst starts with an appreciation based on an open-minded approach to the differences between the 'China Model' of political governance and the liberal democracies of the West. Are so-called 'one-size-fits-all' overriding systems of various flavours of liberal democracy, which is coming under much strain and criticism in the West, the only blueprint for political reform in a country as unique as China? India has sought to go down this path, but how does its modern development compare to China's? For Chinese firms, such economic, political, and geopolitical considerations are relevant in a way unprecedented in modern economic history; hence the emphasis given to them in what is essentially a book on international management. To divorce the international strategies of Chinese firms from their political and cultural context, is to commit a mistake of significant magnitude in an analytical sense.

In China, unlike in Australia or the US, history plays a significant role in the national psyche and in the way the world is viewed, including the role that China should play. This reflects the difference between a civilisation state rather than a modern nation state, covering one-fifth of humanity, with a huge diaspora of at least 50 million, and with a rich history of several thousand years, in contrast to New World countries, which have largely been shaped through immigration over the last 400 years. This is a huge and important difference, which Chinese scholar, Odd Arne Westad (2012) summarised when he wrote: 'History is the most fundamental background on which to understand present-day Chinese foreign relation'. In his excellent book Professor Robert Bickers (2017) emphasises this important perspective: 'China looks out at the twenty-first century through the lens of history'.

The market for books on China seems unlimited, and there is a risk of reader fatigue in producing yet another book on aspects of this fascinating, inspiring, and majestic country. Given that writing a serious book is a long and lonely journey (1,400 hours of writing and a multiple of that in research and reflection), which only adds to the demands already placed on a busy schedule and the patience of loved ones, an important reality check is to ask, 'What does this book add to the sum of knowledge on, insight into, and interest in China?' I spent much time reflecting on this and am satisfied that the reader will not be disappointed. The approach taken in this book is to provide a broad-based context and to argue the case that Chinese firms face significant, if not insurmountable, challenges to the successful prosecution of their overseas expansion. It is hard to think of any other nation in which a broad-based context is so important to understanding the complex environment in which business operates. I am not aware of any book that takes such an approach to an analysis of Chinese firms as they build their presence in the global economy.

This book is aimed at a broad audience, with an objective of contributing to a clear-headed analysis and understanding of the challenges facing Chinese firms in the global economy. Whilst the book is peppered with references to relevant theory and literature, my aim was to write an accessible book, grounded in much practical experience, providing the reader with common sense insights and important contrasts, whilst highlighting the hypocrisy in much of the Western discourse on China. This is not a book intended for academics in search of scholarly rigour, but it will provide a bridge between academia and a wider readership including business leaders, and policy-shapers who wish to reflect and better understand what could be a phenomenal change in the world order and what this might mean for individual nations, particularly (as will become evident in this book) to Australia, my home country. This book will also appeal to the growing legions of China-watchers and general readers who are open-minded, interested in critical thinking, and keen to better understand the increasing profile of Chinese firms in international markets. Are they a threat? To whom? And why?

Every thoughtful business and political leader knows that little sustainable progress is ever made in the international arena until you first put yourself in the shoes of your counterpart and seek to understand them before seeking to be understood. This requires sophisticated qualities of leadership. In this book, I am asking the reader to put themselves in the shoes of the Chinese leaders — both business and political — and seek to understand their context on history, global institutions, the global economy, the evidence of biases against them, and what China needs to do to build a 'moderately prosperous society'. Readers should ask; given its history, its growing contribution to the global economy and its farsighted strategic initiatives, some of which are discussed in this book, is not only reasonable that China and Chinese firms have their fair share of influence and prosperity in the global economy?

About the Author

 **Joseph Healy** is a career international banker who has spent many years working with Chinese firms and has also lived in China. As a member of the Group Executive Committee for a major bank, he held responsibilities for the banks activities in China. A co-founder and co-CEO of Judo Capital, his other activities include being Director of Football Federation Australia (FFA), where he chairs the Football Development Committee. He is also an Adjunct Professor at the University of Queensland Business School and the author of *Corporate Governance and Shareholder Wealth Creation* (2003). He holds an MSc in International Management in China from the School of Oriental and African Studies (SOAS), University of London; an MA in Contemporary Chinese Studies from the University of Nottingham, Ningbo, China, an MSc in Finance from the London Business School, an MBA in banking from Bangor University and an MBA from Henley Management School, University of Reading. He is a member of the Chartered Institute of Bankers (Scotland) and holds five international football caps for Scotland at youth level.

Contents

List of Figures and Tables

Figures

Chapter 2

Chapter 3

Chapter 4

Chapter 5

Tables

List of Acronyms and Abbreviations

CCDI	Central Commission on Discipline Inspection
CCP	Chinese Communist Party
CEO	Chief Executive Officer
CFIUS	Committee on Foreign Investment in the United States
CSA	Country-specific Advantage
EBITDA	Earnings before Interest, Tax, Depreciation, and Amortisation
EVA	Economic Value Added
FDI	Foreign Direct Investment
FLM	Financial Liberation Model
FSA	Firm-specific Advantage
GDP	Gross Domestic Product
GFC	Global Financial Crisis
HBR	Harvard Business Review
IFDI	Inbound Foreign Direct Investment
IMF	International Monetary Fund
M&A	Mergers & Acquisitions
MBA	Master in Business Administration
ME	Management Education
MOFCOM	Ministry of Commerce, People's Republic of China
MP	Member of Parliament
NBS	National Business System
NOPAT	Net Operating Profit After Tax

OBOR	One Belt, One Road
OECD	Organisation for Economic Co-operation and Development
OFDI	Outbound Foreign Direct Investment
PCA	Permanent Court of Arbitration
PM	Prime Minister
POE	Privately Owned Enterprises
PPP	Purchasing Power Parity
PRD	Pearl River Delta
R&D	Research & Development
ROIC	Return on Invested Capital
SOE	State-owned Enterprises
SASAC	State-owned Assets Supervision and Administration Commission
SD	Standard Deviation
SME	Small and Medium-sized Enterprise
S&P	Standard & Poor's
TNI	Trans-Nationality Index
WTO	World Trade Organisation

All references to $ are to US$ unless otherwise stated

Introduction

The scope of the book is both wide ranging and ambitious. I adopt a multidisciplinary approach that weaves together themes from history, contemporary Chinese politics, geopolitics, international relations, economics, finance, strategy, culture, and society, together with the role of management education in developing important capabilities critical to success. The close interrelationship between these themes is pivotal to understanding the central thesis developed in the book. That said, not all readers will want to cover all these themes and read every chapter. For that reason, the chapters are largely self-contained commentaries on specific themes. Certain chapters will interest some readers, whilst other readers may wish to focus on other areas of interest. Chapter 1 is for everyone, as it provides a context in which the globalisation of Chinese firms can be understood, whilst introducing the book's key ideas, historical context, and frameworks. Chapter 2 summarises the facts on Chinese outbound foreign direct investment (OFDI), highlighting some interesting differences between state-owned enterprises (SOEs) and privately owned enterprises (POEs). Chapter 3 should appeal to all readers, as it explores the *five biases* that China and Chinese firms face. This is a significant contribution to the book and will provoke competing interpretations. Chapter 4 is for readers interested in political systems and raises the spectre of how differences in political ideology between 'socialism with Chinese characteristics' and the liberal democratic values dominant in the West can and do influence the way in which Chinese firms are received in the international economy. This could easily be regarded as a bias, but significant global trends are occurring that challenge the notion that all democracies are 'good' and all authoritarian systems 'bad'. Comparing what we are seeing in these different systems today might allow the open-minded reader to question what most in the West have been indoctrinated to regard as an unquestionable truth. In this chapter, I present some comparisons between China and India. Chapter 5 is recommended to all readers, as it introduces cultural factors, including the influence of Confucianism. Culture, because it is both visible and invisible, is often underrated in the craft and science of management and international relations, yet it is crucial for success outside a firm's domestic market, as two case studies presented in this chapter clearly show. Chapter 6 explores the key strategic themes underpinning success for firms as they globalise, and in emphasising a resource-based view of the firm, highlighting the *a priori* contradiction between what theories say and what Chinese firms are doing. An important insight here is how POEs differ from SOEs in their motivation for expanding internationally. Chapter 7, which may appeal more to those with an appetite for finance, discusses how success in international markets should be measured, using a largely financial metric whilst emphasising the pivotal role that banks play within the Chinese financial system as allocators and monitors of capital. The relation of an economy's financial system to its savings and investment decisions is central to understanding the performance of firms and, in China, shows evidence of a repressed financial system with serious market imperfections in how capital is allocated, and risk priced. Chapter 8 is a short chapter for readers interested in the role of management education in developing the capabilities critical to success, including from a Chinese perspective. In Chapter 9, I conclude the principal thesis and arguments, weaving together the themes explored in the book. Throughout, I introduce how some of the primary and much of the secondary research has informed many of the themes explored. A commentary on the design of the primary research is provided in the appendices, for those with an interest in such detail.

In addition to my own research, the reader will find extensive references to the works of others, to both academic and business literature, including many references to *The Economist, The Wall Street Journal* and *Financial Times* (which have been my staple diet for news and insights for over 30 years). I have attributed sources throughout as comprehensively as possible; hopefully, there are no omissions. For any errors that do appear, I sincerely apologise. Given the broad nature of the approach taken, I will inevitably stray into the domain of specialists in certain fields, as some of them will no doubt confirm in due course. Reading the well-considered critical views of others is always a pleasure, never a threat. It is a wonderful opportunity to learn. This is a broad-based book on an important theoretical and practical contemporary issue. Core to the central thesis of this book is that, to understand Chinese firms in the global economy, readers must also understand the unique context that is China and the central role the Chinese Communist Party (CCP) plays through both its visible and invisible hand. Hence, this is a business book that considers the unique and complex socioeconomic, cultural, political and geopolitical environment for business in China.

1

The China Dream

The greatest Chinese dream is the revival of the Chinese nation.

President Xi

As China seeks to become a major actor in the international political, economic, and business community and rebalance its domestic economy growth from investment-led to consumption-led, with a strategic shift to innovation-driven growth, creating a 'moderately prosperous society' by 2021 (the 100-year anniversary of the founding of the Chinese Communist Party), much will depend on the quality of its political and business leaders. In business, the magnitude of the leadership and management challenge is amplified by the fact that China, in an environment dominated by the ideology of Marxism–Leninism and Mao Zedong's 'theory of continuous revolution under the dictatorship of the proletariat', was subject to a self-imposed isolation from the international economy for nearly three decades starting in 1949. In many ways, from 1949 to 1976, China was as mysterious and isolated then as North Korea is today. During that period, it sought to build a self-reliant economic system, largely influenced by the Soviet Union. This influence is evident to those visiting Beijing, who will see, particularly around Tiananmen Square, how Soviet architecture was copied in constructing many government buildings, including The Great Hall of the People. China's isolation was particularly telling from 1966 to

1976, the period of the Cultural Revolution, when there was at least a lost decade if not a generation in terms of intellectual debate and management development. While China was adopting an education system based on Soviet principles, business schools were flourishing in the West, creating generations of well-educated and internationally savvy managers and leaders, educated and inspired by the great management thinkers, such as Michael Porter, Sumantra Ghoshal, David Teece, Clayton Christensen, C.K. Prahalad, Peter Drucker, John Kay, Ram Charan, Kenichi Ohmae, and Gary Hamel, to name only a few.

Since the opening-up reforms introduced by Deng Xiaoping in 1978, Chinese firms have increasingly been engaged in international business, but in a world largely dominated by Western (and some Japanese and Korean) firms. These firms have benefited from first-mover advantage in building international management capabilities since the end of the Second World War, with some Western nations enjoying a long history of cross-border investment. Britain, for example, through the East India Company, can plot an international expansion history back to 1600. The evidence is compelling that, particularly for Britain in the 19th century and the US in the 20th, economic hegemons represent a disproportionate share of cross-border investment. Such nations and firms have generally cultivated the Four Cs of comparative advantage in international markets: *core capabilities, cultural adaptability, competencies of management,* and *country of origin.*

Under the policies of 'reform and opening-up', Deng (1993) acknowledged that 'one important reason for China's backwardness after the industrial revolution in Western countries was its closed-door policy', and that opening the door would enable China 'to make use of capital from foreign countries and of their advanced technology and experience in business management'. Deng's leadership in allowing the impact of Inbound Foreign Direct Investment (IFDI) on China, first through the Special Economic Zones (SEZs) opened in the 1980s and then on most of the coastal cities in the 1990s, cannot be overstated. When an 88-year-old Deng Xiaoping declared during his famous Southern Tour in 1992 that 'to be rich is glorious', his voice rang out loud and was heard by many, unleashing the innate Keynesian 'animal spirits' of the Chinese people, whose ambitions quickly moved from a desire to possess the 'four rounds' (things that go around — a bicycle, a watch, a sewing machine, and a washing machine) to greater things. The fruits of this entrepreneurial drive are clear for all to see when visiting Shenzen, which was not so long ago a rural backwater but is today a dynamic, thriving city of migrants, home to two of China's new breed of multinationals, Huawei and Tencent, and a star amongst the vibrant centres in the Pearl River Delta (PRD). This awakening was a reminder that deep cultures and human nature have a character that cannot be fundamentally changed; Chairman Mao was trying to impose his will on an intractable human and social reality — ultimately an exercise in futility, which he later acknowledged. Even before Mao's death in September 1976, large parts of the countryside had abandoned the planned economy and broken free from the ideological constraints imposed by decades of Maoism and Marxism–Leninism.

In his later years, whilst unwavering on the Four Cardinal Principles (upholding the socialist path, the people's democratic dictatorship, the leadership of the Chinese Communist Party (CCP), and Mao Zedong Thought and Marxism–Leninism), Deng Xiaoping, the great pragmatist ('*it doesn't matter if the cat is black or white, so long as it catches mice,*' '*seek truth from facts*'), did not see the profit motive as an alternative theory to Marxism but a reality of human nature. His leadership pioneered 'socialism with Chinese characteristics', demonstrating an ability to reconcile paradoxes in a China of ideological dogma and helping to transform a command-and-control economy into a dynamic, increasingly hybrid-market-based economy — a 'bird-cage economy' as described by veteran Chinese Communist Party (CCP) leader Chen Yun: the planned economy/political system was the cage, and the bird was the market economy — a wonderful, thought-provoking metaphor.

The result has been an economy growing three times faster than global GDP for almost 40 years and, although currently slower, continuing to evolve and grow. It is now the second-largest economy in nominal GDP terms and the largest when using a measure called 'purchasing power parity (PPP)' that adjusts for differences in local prices. China's GDP grew from $177 billion in 1978 to nearly $12 trillion in 2016, an unprecedented growth of over 6000%. The 'slower' forecasted economic growth of 6.5–7.0% in 2017–2018 must be put in perspective: a 6.5% GDP growth will see the economy grow by $750 billion in 2017 compared to growth of $500 billion in 2007, when the pace of growth was 14%. A $750 billion growth in 1 year is equal to almost half the size of the entire Australian economy. On top of this impressive economic growth story, China, unlike the traditional global powers, is showing international leadership through the One Belt, One Road (OBOR) strategy, which will transform the economies of many countries through Central Asia and the Middle East to Europe. The strategic visions shown by China, which I discuss in Chapter 4, have not been seen in the world since the more modest Marshall Plan in Western Europe post World War II. It has the potential to be a defining geo-economic strategy.

The impressive economic headlines disguise the fact that China is a contradictory and complex economy of significant regional variations and is a real laggard in GDP per capita terms. China's GDP per capita is less than a third that of the US, the UK, and Australia, suggesting that China's impressive growth still has considerable runway ahead if it is to avoid the middle-income trap that has afflicted many developing economies. Readers are reminded that GDP is a narrow measure of economic development, and this is particularly true of China (US Senator Robert Kennedy once said that GDP measures everything but tells us nothing). Illustrative of China's uniqueness, however, is that never has one of the world's largest economies been a developing economy. In almost four decades, China has achieved two historic transformations: from a rural, agricultural society to an urban, industrial one and from a command economy to one embracing many market-based principles and that is becoming increasingly international in its outlook. Chen Yun's 'birdcage economy' has seen the cage expand as the bird has grown; the difference today, to extend the metaphor, is that the bird is flying outside the physical cage when it enters international markets, or is it?

Evidence of 'the bird flying' includes the many changes seen in China in recent years. One important change is the switch from being a net importer to becoming a net exporter of capital. The period since the beginning of the 2008 Global Financial Crisis (GFC) created an extraordinary strategic opportunity for Chinese firms to accelerate their internationalisation by acquiring businesses in the West, with so many firms impacted by the crisis and the economic slowdown and the resultant asset price deflation. The significance of this in the global economy is not to be underestimated, even though China's stock of Outbound Foreign Direct Investment (OFDI) is still small compared to leading Western nations. There is much merit in the argument that China's economic future will largely determine the world's future, hence, in part, the anxiety so many Westerners are feeling regarding China. The globalisation of Chinese firms is a reality that needs to be better understood, free from the popular rhetoric (biases and myths) that so often frames discourse and crowds out open-minded, intelligent thinking.

Politics plays an important role in business. This is particularly true concerning the globalisation of Chinese firms, which cannot be completely divorced from domestic politics and CCP's agenda (but it would be equally wrong to overstate this influence). In 1999, the Chinese political leadership actively encouraged Chinese firms, mostly State-owned Enterprises (SOEs), to 'go global', or *zou chu qu*, which led to a surge in international expansion, often with the benefit of a copious supply of cheap labour, subsidised bank loans, government subsidies, and soft budget constraints (whereby financial outcome metrics and performance evaluation consequences were loosely connected; if you missed your targets, so what?). The progress since the 1990s in integrating with the international economy has been impressive, particularly since China joined the World Trade Organisation (WTO) in 2001. Whilst much of the early expansion was into peripheral, less-competitive developing economies in Africa and Latin America, Chinese firms have been entering developed economies and coming up against well-entrenched domestic and global competitors. Chinese Vice-Premier Wu Bangguo commented in 1998:

> International economic comparisons show that if a country has several large companies or groups it will be assured of maintaining a certain market share and a position in the international economic order. America, for example, relies on General Motors, Boeing, Du Pont and a batch of other multinational companies. Japan relies on six large enterprise groups and Korea relies on ten large commercial groupings. In the same way now and in the next century our nation's position in the international economic order will be to a large extent determined by the position of our nation's large enterprises and groups. (Nolan, 2014)

In 2016, for the first time in history, the flow of China's OFDI came close to matching the IFDI, and it appears to be only a matter of time before China's OFDI exceeds the IFDI, both in flow and stock, even ignoring the significant impact of the OBOR strategy. This is a historic and symbolic development in the modern history of China and is congruent with the aspirations explicit in the future-oriented vision of the 'Chinese Dream of the great rejuvenation of the Chinese nation (Xi, 2014) (or *zhonghua minzu weida fuxing*): a strong China as an influential actor in the League of Nations. As Wang Jianlin, Chairman of Dalian Wanda and one of China's richest tycoon said, 'If companies do not globalise, China won't become powerful'.[1]

China, a hugely proud and patriotic nation, which, under the leadership of President Xi, has become increasingly nationalistic, subtly promoting a historical sense of superiority and grave injustice inflicted by foreigners. These injustices were epitomised by the 'unequal treaties', which saw the integrity of China's sovereignty degraded by a number of foreign settlements or concessions as they were known, which discriminated against the Chinese, treating them as second-class citizens in their own land (an example of this

---

[1] *The Economist*, Crossing the River, June 10, 2017, p. 61.

was a sign on the entrance to a park in Shanghai which proclaimed *Huaren yu gou bude rune: Chinese and Dogs Not Admitted*). This sense of national pride is based partly on the fact that China has a long history of international trade (some 3,000 years) and was the source of innovation in papermaking, printing, the compass, wheelbarrows, horse collars, telescopes, clocks, and gunpowder, all of which have made an important contribution to global economic development. The 17th century British philosopher Francis Bacon famously said that the most important influences on the world were based on three great innovations: printing, gunpowder, and the compass. What he didn't know when making this declaration was that all three were discovered in China (Winchester, 2008). Through this lens, the rise of China in the 21st century can be viewed as not a new development but the re-establishing of a previously held position; a reclaiming of its heritage as an inventive nation. We should not forget that it was only in 1820 when China, the 'Middle Kingdom' (*Zhongguo*) as it was known, produced over 30% of global GDP, exceeding the GDP of the US and Europe combined (Maddison, 2006). In so many ways, China may be returning to the position in the global economy it held before the industrial revolution: not the rise of a new power but a renaissance. In this context, the commitment to OBOR will be a pivotal strategy, not just because of its economic significance but also because of its symbolism and contrast to the West, which finds itself inward looking and, in so many ways, in a state of crisis, lacking a cohesive global strategy. More on this in Chapter 4.

China's decline as an economic power began in the 17th and 18th centuries, largely due to its isolation from the rest of the world and a sense of superiority, which caused it to become complacent about the innovations that were taking place during the industrial revolution. Harvard University Professor David Landes (1998) suggests that: 'China had long slipped into technological and scientific torpor, coasting along on previous gains and losing speed as talent yielded to gentility... so years passed and the decades and the centuries. Europe left China far behind'. This complacency and sense of superiority can be traced back to an Imperial time, before the 'Century of Humiliation' that began with the Opium Wars in 1839, with China then subject to invasion, unequal treaties, and foreign domination[2] — to a period when China was surrounded by vassal states that paid tribute to the Middle Kingdom. Further afield were Barbarians whose countries were so distant from China that they were deemed less than worthy. China's sense of self meant that it showed little interest in the rest of the world, as Britain's Lord Macartney discovered when leading a trade mission to China in 1793 on behalf of King George III. Macartney found the Chinese dismissive of the many wonders he brought, viewing his goods more as tribute than as trade and insisting that he kowtow to the Emperor, the 'Son of Heaven' and master of 'All Under Heaven', or return home. China saw nothing of worth in the world outside its domain. In his excellent book, *The Collision of Two Civilizations* (1993), Alain Peyrefitte describes the meeting as the 'collision of two planets, with the British and Chinese discovering two mutually refined civilisations, yet incompatible cultures, one celestial and lunar; the other with its feet firmly on the ground — mercantile, scientific, and industrial'.

Commanding Heights of Global Business

In a contemporary context, business — as are culture, sports, media, education, foreign policy, and other soft-power pursuits — is one of the levers that will help project China's aspirations in global political economy. In sports, President Xi is placing great emphasis on building China's credentials in international football ('soccer' to some), where Chinese investors have been acquiring interests in European and Australian clubs. Parallels can be made with the rise of US multinationals such as McDonald's, Coca-Cola, IBM, General Motors, General Electric (GE), Boeing, Microsoft, Citibank, Google, Amazon, and Apple, and how they played a role in building a global network promoting American ideals, culture, and economic might. GE now operates in 180 countries. Citibank does business in 160 countries,

---

[2]A chronology of the 'Century of Humiliation' is provided in Appendix 5 given the significance of that period to the psyche of modern China. Appendix 6 provides a chronology of key events in China since 1911.

IBM is in 170 countries, and McDonald's is in 119. These firms, through deep experience, understand the importance of knowing the 'rules of the game' when entering foreign markets and what it takes to succeed. They share a strong 'administrative heritage'.

The 'commanding heights' of the global business system, as Professor Nolan argues, are occupied almost entirely by firms from high-income countries. Whilst Chinese firms are second only to US firms in terms of market capitalisation within the *FT 500* and *Fortune 500* large-firm index, these firms are mostly SOEs and owe their size to the benefits of a protected, often monopolistic, position within their domestic market rather than to their management competencies, cultural adaptability, or competitive advantage-based success in the global economy. As discussed in Chapter 7, many of the SOEs are a reminder that being big does not mean being successful. As a measure of the power of US-domiciled global firms, the share of nominal GDP among the *Fortune 100* largest American companies rose from 33% in 1994 to 46% by 2013.[3] Thus, those who point to the fact that Chinese firms in the decade up to 2016 increased their representation in the *Fortune 500* from 20 to 103 (13 of those entering in 2016 alone) as evidence of the rise of China in the global arena materially overstate their case (Table 1). They are focusing on what is *counted* and losing sight of what *counts* in defining truly international firms. I come back to this theme in Chapter 3.

Chinese Ambition

Despite being latecomers, the magnitude of the task ahead has not perturbed Chinese authorities from identifying the need to create globally competitive firms as a policy objective. In his speech to the 18th CCP Congress, in 2012, President Hu Jintao said:

> Chinese companies should expand their overseas presence at a faster rate, enhance their cooperation in an international environment and develop a number of world-class multinational corporations.

---

[3] *The Economist*, The rise of superstar: Special report, September 17, 2016.

Table 1: *Fortune 500* Top-15 Nations

Nation	2006	2016	Change
US	168	134	−34
China	20	103	+83
Japan	70	52	−18
France	38	29	−9
Germany	35	28	−7
UK	38	26	−12
South Korea	12	15	+3
Switzerland	13	15	+2
Netherlands	15	12	−3
Canada	14	11	−3
Spain	9	9	—
Italy	10	9	−1
Australia	8	8	—
Taiwan	3	7	+4
Brazil	4	7	+3

Source: Fortune 500, 2016 (www.fortune.com/fortune 500).

China has yet to develop global giants, largely because of the youth of many of its firms. Nevertheless, in a relatively short period, internationally focused firms such as Hangzhou-based and NYSE-listed Alibaba and Shenzhen-based Tencent, Baidu, China National Chemical, Geely, Huawei, JD.Com, Dalian Wanda, Anbang, ZTE, Fosun, Hisense, Lenovo, Xiaomi, HNA, Suntech, Goodbaby, and TCL have emerged, and others will follow. Many of these firms are seeking to break the mould of the Chinese firms that largely adopted a 'me too', copycat and sometimes counterfeits lower-cost strategy. Several firms, such as Huawei, Haier, HNA, and Alibaba, are seeking to move from brawn to brains, from quantity to quality, and to build global brands aimed not just at an increasingly vast Internet consumer-savvy domestic middle-class, where international brands have huge appeal, but also at international markets as China seeks to build national brand equity.

The Chinese government's 'Made in China 2025' initiative aimed at achieving a comprehensive upgrade in Chinese industry is modelled on Germany's 'industry 4.0 plan' (Kennedy, 2015). The 2025 plan identifies 10 strategic industries as priorities: (1) new advanced information technology; (2) automated machine tools and robotics; (3) aerospace and aeronautical equipment; (4) maritime equipment and high-tech shipping; (5) modern rail transport; (6) new energy vehicle and equipment; (7) power equipment; (8) agricultural equipment; (9) new materials; and (10) biopharma and advanced medical products. The 2025 initiative also calls for greater emphasis on management capabilities in areas such as human resource management, risk management, and operational efficiency, as well as on Chinese firms' understanding of different cultures, a positive measure to address deeply ingrained perception-based biases impacting Chinese firms. The handicap of existing biases creates management challenges for firms such as Xiaomi, who have set the goal of overtaking Apple and Samsung in the global smartphone market by providing a lower-cost and higher-quality alternative. Xiaomi's CEO has publicly stated that *Xiaomi's mission is to build China's first global consumer brand and change the world's view of Chinese products.*[4] I discuss these biases in Chapter 3.

Like Xiaomi, Haier, Huawei, JD.Com, Tencent, Goodbaby, and Alibaba, some of the new Chinese firms may have the potential to be global disruptors, driving business model revolutions with unique disruptor strategies and perhaps developing premium brands, benefitting from the impact that technology and virtually connected networks are having on entry barriers, industry, and market structures. The Western world often seems preoccupied with Silicon Valley for technology-based innovation and risks overlooking what is happening in China and its so-called 'Silicon Dragons', with firms such as Internet giant Alibaba, Baidu, Tencent-owned WeChat, smartphone manufacturer Xiaomi, taxi-hailing firm Didi Kuaidi, peer-to-peer lending platform Lufax, and food delivery and

---

[4] *Wall Street Journal*, China's new phone giant takes aim at the world, June 9, 2015, pp. 12–13.

movie ticket group Meituan-Dianping all growing into multi-billion valued enterprises. Some of these firms have the theoretical potential for overseas expansion, being no longer constrained by the barriers that geography once created to new markets. For example, Haier, an SOE on the verge of bankruptcy in 1984, is today the largest producer of white goods in the world. Driven by the narrowness and rigidity of the bank-dominated financial system, the fastest-growing fintech sector in the world is in China and was worth $1.8 trillion at the end of 2015 (Mckinsey & Co., 2016). Many of the mobile apps widely used in China are at a level of sophistication not yet evident in the West, with capabilities that seem destined to shape developments in the West. As many Australian boards plan their once-in-a-business cycle visit to Silicon Valley, which has become a must-do, they are well advised to look closer home for market- and industry-shaping innovations.

Competitive Advantage in Global Markets

Of course, the financial capability and domestic prowess of many Chinese firms do not necessarily equate to management capability in international markets. High-performing firms in international markets, no matter their sector, have the following characteristics in common: (1) a strong management that is clear on its strategy and is able to communicate it easily to employees, customers, investors and stakeholders and then execute rigorously; (2) the ability to innovate, be it in technology, product design, or customer relations; and (3) the ability to successfully deploy its capabilities internationally, through either firm-specific advantages (FSA) or country-specific advantages (CSA). Applying this lens to several high-profile Chinese firms shows that the logic behind many international expansion strategies is not yet clear. Consider three high-profile examples.

First, consider HNA Group, headquartered in Hainan, southern China. It began as a regional airline and then from 2015 to 2017 turned itself into a conglomerate by borrowing and spending $42.5 billion on over 70 international investments since 2008, including a stake in the Hilton hotel group, a stake in German giant Deutsche

Bank, and a 25% stake in US asset-management firm Old Mutual. It acquired New York financial firm CIT Group for $10 billion and paid $6 billion for California-based Ingram Micro, the world's largest distributor of technology products. It owns 13% of Virgin Australia together with 15 other airlines including in Brazil and South Africa; the list goes on. In many of HNA's deals, borrowing has been secured on the assets of the acquired company — a process known in Chinese as 'a snake swallowing an elephant'. Adding to the complexity of HNA is a lack of knowledge about who its largest shareholders are, together with a complex corporate structure, in which close to 30% of the firms' equity is held by an obscure New York-registered non-profit trust called 'Hainan Cihang Charity Foundation'. The remaining 70% of the ownership resides with Hainan Airlines Holding and 18 individuals whose identity is confidential. According to the *Financial Times*,[5] HNA controls 11 peer-to-peer lending platforms in China, including the largest, Jubao Internet Technology, through which it has raised RMB 682 million at interest rates between 7% and 12%, with a product duration ranging from 20 days to 1 year. Most of the liabilities are guaranteed by HNA or its subsidiaries, but critics have pointed to the opaque nature of HNA's finances and concerns that short-duration debt is funding its expansion. These concerns grow louder, even though HNA's CEO has stated a goal of building the firm into one of the world's top 10 biggest businesses.[6] In 2017, HNA generated two-thirds of its revenues from outside China and had 45,000 in the US.

The second example is Anbang, which started as an auto insurer but, through a range of acquisitions, including the $2 billion acquisition of the Waldorf Astoria Hotel in New York (some of those attempted between 2015 and 2017 are summarised in Table 2), is now a major conglomerate controlling some $250–300 billion in assets, having made international acquisitions worth $17 billion

---

[5] *Financial Times*, China probe shines light on top dealmakers, June 23, 2017, p. 17.
[6] *Fortune*, You've never heard of HNA group — here's why you will, August 2017, pp. 60–67.

Table 2:   Anbang Selected Acquisition Announcements, 2015–2017

Target	$billion	Country	Status	Industry
DoubleTree by Hilton	0.39	Holland	Completed	Dining & Lodging
Kushner	0.40	US	Not pursued	Property
Strategic Hotels & Resorts	5.50	US	Completed	Property
Starwood Hotels & Resorts	15.49	US	Withdrawn	Dining & Lodging
Heron Tower, London	1.17	UK	Not pursued	Property
Waldorf Astoria	1.95	US	Completed	Dining & Lodging

Sources: Dealogic; Bloomberg; *The Economist*, (2017, p. 56).

since 2014. Like HNA, Anbang uses short-term funding instruments to finance long-term investments. Anbang is headed by Wu Xiaohui, who is married to a granddaughter of Deng Xiaoping. Despite this powerful heritage, in early 2018, Mr Wu was charged with embezzlement and fundraising fraud, and the Chinese authorities seized control of Anbang, claiming that the business had 'illegal business operations which may seriously endanger the company's solvency.'[7]

The third example is Fosun, founded in the early 1990s by a group of alumni from Fudan University. It began by investing in property before diversifying into mining and pharmaceuticals. Co-founder and Chairman Guo Guangchang styles himself as the 'Warren Buffet of China'. Fosun is now a sprawling conglomerate, having spent just under $40 billion in acquisitions between 2010 and 2017, including for the purchase of French leisure company Club Med, Canadian entertainment group Cirque du Soleil, an 86% stake in Indian pharmaceutical Gland Pharma for $1.1 billion, and second-tier English football team Wolverhampton Wanderers. The question of corporate governance was highlighted, however, when Fosun abandoned its bid for the UK merchant bank Kleinwort Benson after receiving financial transparency demands from the UK regulators.

The FSAs or core capabilities that HNA, Anbang and Fosun bring to many of their investments are not obvious; thus, the prospects for

---

[7] *Financial Times*, China seizes Anbang in latest move to curb dealmakers, February 23, 2018, p. 1.

success are not clear when assessed against conventional frameworks for international strategy, as discussed in Chapters 6 and 7. These firms are not unique in the Chinese context; firms such as Zhejian Geely Holding Group, a conglomerate based in Hangzhou, with a competency in car manufacturing (it owns Volvo, has a stake in Daimler[8] and controls British sports car brand Lotus), announced in 2017 that it was seeking to buy Danish Bank and Saxo Bank. Another example is Legend, the largest shareholder in Lenovo computers, which acquired a 90% stake in European bank, Banque Internationale a Luxembourg.[9] I discuss in Chapter 7 some of the risks associated with the financing of some of China's leading international firms.

Management Capabilities

Given the relative newness of Chinese firms to owning and operating assets in foreign markets and the absence of their familiar ecosystems and networks (*guanxi*) in many markets, legitimate questions can be asked about the ability of Chinese management to successfully run international businesses. The background and experience of management does matter to the essential human capital of a firm. The psychological influences, for example, of the Cultural Revolution on managers in their mid-40s and older may influence how business is conducted, relationships and trust established, and worldviews developed. Whilst China has a growing stock of university-qualified people to take up roles requiring basic skill levels, the stock of key managerial, financial, project management, and international experience is limited. China expert Professor David Shambaugh (2012) summed up the situation:

> The Achilles heel of Chinese multinationals is human resources. Multilingual and multicultural managers are few and far between.... as a result, Chinese students are flooding into foreign MBA programs as well as business schools in China...but classroom training

---

[8] *Financial Times*, Is Chinese state behind Geely's Daimler Swoop? February 28, 2018, p. 17.

[9] *The Economist*, Chinese acquisitions, freezers to finance, October 7, 2017, p. 73.

alone will not suffice because there is no substitute for extensive international experience.

In developing management capabilities, management education has an important role to play in the success of the international economy, but it is not enough. The emphasis on education does not imply that all successful international business leaders must have had some formal management education. There are many exceptions, such as Haier Chairman and CEO Zhang Ruimin, who ended his formal education at 17 and has gone on to create a world-leading electrical goods business, including the acquisition of New Zealand's Fisher & Paykel. Others, such as ZTE's Hau Weigui and Wanxiang's Lu Guanqiu, started on the factory floor. However, given the scale of the management and leadership challenges Chinese firms face in the international economy, management education can play a critical role in shaping China's future, as it has done so profoundly in the West, where, for example, around two-fifths of *Fortune 500* CEOs hold an MBA or equivalent.[10] A simple insight into the management challenge China faces is provided by the fact that, in 2016, US universities produced over three-times the number of masters-qualified business graduates than did universities in China. Of course, this simple quantitative measurement says nothing about the qualitative aspects of the management education experience, which I discuss in Chapter 8.

---

[10] *The Economist,* Campus versus beach, October 15, 2016.

2

The Facts on Chinese OFDI

We commit ourselves to growing an open global economy to share opportunities and interests through opening-up and achieving win–win outcomes.

President Xi, Davos, 2017

Generally, investments in other countries can be made in two different ways — FDI and portfolio investment. The difference between FDI and portfolio (or financial) investment can be understood in terms of whether the investment gives the purchaser any control over the use of the asset. A small minority shareholding gives no control, a larger shareholding might give some control, and a majority shareholding gives much control. FDI implies that there is some control over the foreign assets or businesses in which the investment is made. FDI can further be split into investment in established businesses or assets, and investment in construction such as roads, pipelines, and other forms of infrastructure. I discuss this distinction below. Portfolio investment, by contrast, includes debt and equity securities, money market instruments, and financial derivatives. Portfolio investment differs from FDI in that, whilst the investment provides the owner with a claim on the cash flows from the investment, it does not provide a 'voice' in the management of the investment. This is an important distinction. Another important distinction is that a firm can internationalise its operations through

17

exports, which is the most common way to reach foreign markets at an early stage of internationalisation, but this is not FDI, which is the most developed stage of internationalisation. Outbound Foreign Direct Investment (OFDI) is now the most significant path by which Chinese firms are internationalising, whilst China continues to be a prolific exporter, with 14% of the global exports market, the highest any country has reached since the US in 1968.[1]

FDI is defined by the Organisation for Economic Co-operation and Development (OECD, 2012) as:

> a category of investment that reflects the objective of establishing a lasting interest by a resident enterprise in one economy in an enterprise that is resident in an economy other than that of the direct investor….The direct or indirect ownership of 10% or more of the voting power of an enterprise resident in one economy by an investor resident in another economy is evidence of such a relationship.

China has evolved from a trade-focused to a foreign investment-led nation, as evidenced by the fact that it is the most active international country amongst developing nations. In 2000, Chinese firms spent approximately $1 billion on OFDI. Since then, there has been a 30% year-on-year growth (Figure 1), and, in 2016, OFDI exceeded $175 billion (a record-breaking $227 billion of intended investments were announced but not all were completed).[2] In aggregate, China's total OFDI at the end of 2016 exceeded $1.4 trillion. Whilst this is impressive growth, the stock of China's outbound investment is small compared to that of many Western nations, at less than one-tenth of the stock of overseas investment of the UK or Europe and less than one-twentieth of the US, whose stock of OFDI exceeds $5 trillion. China's stock of OFDI as a proportion of GDP stands at close to 8%, compared to 38% for the US, 20% for Japan, 47% for Germany, and 32% for Australia.

---

[1]*The Economist*, Does China play fair? September 23, 2017, p. 9.
[2]*Wall Street Journal*, Capital curbs hit China deal spree, January 30, 2017.

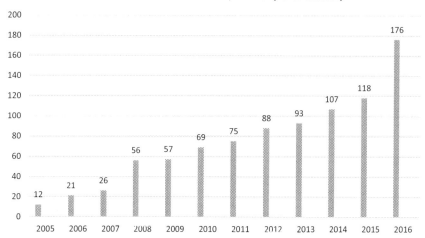

Figure 1:   Chinese Overseas Investment, 2005–2016

Source: Heritage Foundation/American Enterprise Institute, www.aei.org/china-global-investment-tracker.

While early Chinese investments focused on energy and natural resource assets in developing countries, the destination of Chinese OFDI in recent years has been businesses in developed economies, with the US the largest recipient of investment over the past decade, with a record $45.6 billion invested in 2016,[3] almost triple the $15 billion for 2015 ($11.9 billion in 2014) and almost doubling the stock of Chinese investments in the US to $154 billion, despite greater political scrutiny and sensitivity (US firms have invested $228 billion in China since 2000) (Figure 2). The largest Chinese acquisition in the US was the $6.5 billion purchase by HNA of the US software distributor Ingram Micro following the $5.6 billion purchase of General Electric's appliance division by Haier. Much of the growth in the US has occurred since 2012. Until that year, Australia had been the number-one destination over the previous 10 years as state-owned enterprises (SOEs) acquired natural resources, energy, and agricultural assets. New Zealand's share of Chinese investment,

---

[3]*Financial Times*, Surge in Chinese corporate investment into the US, January 2, 2017.

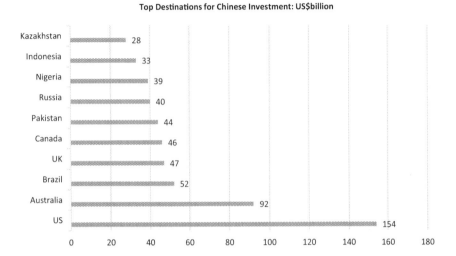

Top Destinations for Chinese Investment: US$billion

Figure 2:   Top Destinations for Chinese Investment, 2005–2016

Source: Heritage Foundation/American Enterprise Institute, www.aei.org/china-global-investment-tracker.

whilst growing, remains less than 2%. The European Union (EU) saw a 76% increase in Chinese investment to $37 billion in 2016 (with Chinese acquisitions by EU firms at $8 billion). The UK had been the favourite European country to invest in by a significant margin over Germany and France, but, in 2016, investments in Germany reached $11.2 billion, up from $1.3 billion in 2015. The UK now accounts for 23.3% of all Chinese investment in the EU (2000–2016), (Figure 2), while Germany accounts for 18.5%, Italy 12.7%, and France 11.3%.[4] Another focus of Chinese investment has been Africa, given its endowment of natural resources, where there has been a focus on construction-based investment. China has invested in 34 African countries, with Nigeria being the largest recipient. Ethiopia and Algeria have attracted more than $15 billion, with Angola and South Africa each drawing almost $10 billion. As discussed below, Pakistan has been a major recipient of Chinese

---

[4]*Financial Times,* Chinese investment in the EU dwarfs flow from the other way, January 11, 2017.

investment with the implication of geopolitical considerations. Political tensions help explain why China has invested almost as much in Mongolia ($1.4 billion) as it has in Japan ($1.6 billion), although, as noted below, Japan is a favoured destination for privately owned enterprises (POE) OFDI. Whilst Chinese firms are actively buying technology and consumer assets in Europe and the US, their lack of acquisitions in Korea and Japan is noteworthy.

Media headlines tend to focus on the big-ticket transactions, but they are not representative of the majority of OFDI. Most Chinese-led international mergers and acquisitions (M&As) are middle market, with the median deal size over the 3 years up to 2016 at around $30 million (McKinsey & Co., 2017).

Investment and Construction

Investments in existing assets and in construction projects are discreet activities. Table 1 splits China's investments into these two categories.

Table 1:　Chinese OFDI: Split between Investment and Construction

Sector	Investment ($billion)	Construction ($billion)	Total ($billion)
Energy	325	270	595
Transport	71	198	269
Metals	118	29	147
Property	80	66	146
Technology	58	17	75
Finance	61	—	61
Agriculture	34	17	51
Tourism	32	4	36
Entertainment	32	2	34
Chemical	11	8	19
Others	36	16	52
Total	**858**	**628**	**1,486**

Source: Heritage Foundation/American Enterprise Institute, www.aei.org/china-global-investment-tracker.

Table 2: Construction by Country Since 2005

Country	Investment ($billion)
Pakistan	33.8
Nigeria	31.1
Saudi Arabia	23.6
Algeria	22.7
Ethiopia	20.7
Indonesia	20.3
Malaysia	20.3
Venezuela	16.2
Vietnam	16.2
Bangladesh	15.9
Sub total	**220.8**
Total for all countries	**627.9**

Source: Heritage Foundation/American Enterprise Institute,
www.aei.org/china-global-investment-tracker.

The destination of China's construction project investments is virtually all in the developing world with little construction investment in Western economies, as illustrated in Table 2.

Pakistan, under the China–Pakistan Economic Corridor (CPEC) launched in 2015, has been a major source of Chinese infrastructure investment in power plants, roads, railways, pipelines, and a deepwater port in the coastal region of Gwadar.

The underlying asset nature of Chinese outbound investment is changing. There has been a growing emphasis on food, agriculture, hoteling, travel, entertainment, consumer products, chemicals, advanced manufacturing, services, and technology, much of this driven by the consumption demands of a rising middle class. Europe's energy, automotive, food, and real estate sectors have attracted a growing flow of Chinese investment. This is illustrated by Table 3, which highlights a range of deals completed by the EU in 2016, consistent with a bias for M&A as a method of market entry.

In 2015, Chinese firms completed more than 100 M&A in the US, at a value of $15 billion, including the purchase of the Waldorf Astoria

Table 3:   Biggest China–EU Deals in 2016

Chinese buyer	Target	Price ($billion)	Industry	Country
Tencent	Supercell	6.7	Gaming	Finland
Midea	Kuka	4.4	Robotics	Germany
Consortium	Global Switch	2.8	Telecom	UK
HNA	Avolon	2.3	Aviation	Ireland
Ctrip	Skyscanner	1.7	Travel	UK
Beijing Enterprises	EEW Energy	1.4	Energy	Germany
Shandong Ruyi	SMCP Group	1.3	Fashion	France
Wanda AMC	Odeon & UCI	1.1	Entertainment	UK

Source: Rhodium; Metrics.

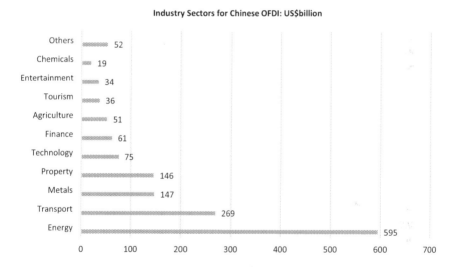

Industry Sectors for Chinese OFDI: US$billion

Others — 52
Chemicals — 19
Entertainment — 34
Tourism — 36
Agriculture — 51
Finance — 61
Technology — 75
Property — 146
Metals — 147
Transport — 269
Energy — 595

Figure 3:   Industry Sectors for Chinese Overseas Investment, 2005–2016
Source: Heritage Foundation/American Enterprise Institute, www.aei.org/china-global-investment-tracker.

Hotel in New York. The total value of bids for US firms by would-be Chinese acquirers was $16.4 billion in 2015, compared with $32 billion in Europe. In 2016, bids for the US firms exceeded $55 billion, while Europe attracted $65 billion, including the $44 billion bid by ChemChina for Swiss chemicals and seed group Syngenta (Figure 3).

Table 4:   Balance between China's Inflows and Outflows of FDI ($billion)

	2000	2005	2010	2015
IFDI	40	72	115	135
OFDI	1	12	69	118
Net	39	60	46	17
IFDI stock	193	272	588	1,220
OFDI stock	28	57	317	1,010
Net	165	215	271	210

Source: UNCTAD (2016) Annex, Tables 1–4.

Table 4 shows a significant increase in OFDI flows compared to Inbound Foreign Direct Investment (IFDI). Consequently, the stock of OFDI has grown from $28 billion in 2000 to $1 trillion in 2015 (and $1.4 trillion in 2016).

The data on OFDI (as with much official Chinese data) can suffer from inaccuracies and may be distorted due to the presence of Hong Kong, which accounts for the lion's share of OFDI on face value. What the data do not indicate is the degree of 'round tripping', or reverse flows from Hong Kong back to China. Round tripping is a direct investment by a Chinese firm into another jurisdiction such as Hong Kong, which is then imported back into China to enjoy preferential investment treatment. Whilst notoriously difficult to quantify, estimates suggest that approximately 40% of all flows to Hong Kong from China end up being reinvested back into China as IFDI. Another complexity in determining the ultimate destination of investment is the use by Chinese investors of tax havens such as the Virgin and Cayman Islands and Western Samoa, where the ultimate destination of the investment is unclear. This distortion reflects the fact that Ministry of Commerce, People's Republic of China (MOFCOM) requires exporters to register the first (not final) destination of their cross-border transactions and not consider reverse flows. Round-trip FDI has a limited effect on net capital inflows, as the imported capital will ultimately cancel out the capital that is exported.

POE's OFDI

The above data include both SOEs and POEs. An interesting perspective is to look at the nature of POE's OFDI: whilst SOEs have historically been the major investors in OFDI, POEs are the major participants in terms of the number of OFDI projects and, as noted in Table 5, are accounted for a growing share of the value of OFDI.

The growth in private sector investment is an important development, with POEs likely to exceed SOEs in international investment, reflecting the growing role played by POEs in the Chinese economy, as Nicholas Lardy describes in his excellent book *Markets over Mao* (2014).

The expanding roles of POEs and broad-market forces have driven much of China's economic growth, including its employment and exports, where POEs now account for over 33% of all exports, up from less than 10% in 2000. This is not surprising, as POEs are leveraging China's Country-Specific Advantage (CSA) abundance of low-cost labour. What is perhaps more surprising is that POEs, and often Small and Medium-sized Enterprises (SMEs), despite frequently lacking access to capital and the benefits of scale, are increasingly prominent in OFDI. POEs in China create more than 75% of jobs and account for more than 50% of GDP but receive less than 5% of bank lending. Theory would suggest that POEs should

Table 5: Private Sector Share of OFDI Since 2010

Year	Percentage of total OFDI (%)
2010	8.3
2011	11.1
2012	14.0
2013	24.4
2014	23.9
2015	32.5
2016	47.9

Source: Heritage Foundation/American Enterprise Institute, www.aei.org/china-global-investment-tracker.

Table 6:   Industrial Sectors for POE's OFDI

Industry	No. of companies	Ratio (%)
Food, beverage, and tobacco	48	7.09
Textiles	132	19.5
Leather	26	3.8
Wood products	12	1.8
Pulp, paper, publishing, and printing	16	2.4
Coal, refined petroleum products, and nuclear fuel	—	—
Chemicals and synthetic fibres	58	8.6
Rubber and plastic products	38	5.6
Non-metallic mineral products	30	4.4
Basic metals and fabricated metal products	56	8.3
Machinery and equipment	123	18.2
Electrical and optical equipment	56	8.3
Manufacture of transport equipment	24	3.6
Other manufacturing equipment	58	8.6
Sum	677	100.0

Source: Wen and Liyun (2015, p. 147).

first grow by building scale in their domestic market before venturing overseas. The bird in the birdcage has grown in a way that the builders of the cage could not have foreseen, with firms (many of them SMEs) from Zhejiang, Guangdong, Jiangsu, Fujian, and Shandong accounting for close to 50% of the POE's OFDI (Wen and Liyun, 2015).

The POEs' focus on the OFDI sector differs from the aggregate data shown above (see Table 6).

Geographically, based on the number of POEs, there is a greater bias towards Asian markets, which account for 47.6%, compared to 33% in the European Union (primarily France, Germany, and Italy), with only 2.7% choosing Australia, in sharp contrast to the aggregate data (see Table 7).

Chinese firms are playing an increasing role in Asia Pacific M&A, with their volume tripling from $259 billion in 2013 to $735 billion in 2015. In 2016, 7 in every 10 of the largest cross-regional

Table 7: Main Destination of POE's OFDI

Country/region	No. of companies	Ratio (%)
US	110	18.0
Japan	101	16.4
France	75	12.3
Hong Kong	72	11.8
Germany	64	10.5
Republic of Korea	50	8.1
Vietnam	37	6.0
Italy	27	4.4
UAE	19	3.1
Australia	17	2.7

Source: Wen and Liyun (2015, p. 148).

acquisitions were made by Chinese firms.[5] The bias towards Asian markets among POEs shows that cultural proximity is an important factor. POEs have invested in countries that include large ethnic Chinese populations, such as Vietnam, Korea, Hong Kong, Thailand, Singapore, and Indonesia.

When entering Europe or North America, however, the investment method of POEs shows a strong bias (72%) towards Greenfield wholly owned subsidiary rather than M&A (16%) or joint venture (12%) (Figure 4).

The statistics are broadly similar for Africa: 74% wholly owned subsidiary and 26% M&A, but there is no appetite for joint ventures (Figure 5).

In summary, whilst the growth in China's OFDI has been both impressive and, in the eyes of some in the West, alarming, it remains small compared to the US and many European countries. Some analysts forecast that the scale of Chinese OFDI will double in stock terms to $2 trillion by 2020[6] despite occasional attempts by the CCP

---

[5]*China's Increasing Outbound M&A*, JP Morgan Insights, 2016.
[6]*Financial Times*, China to become one of the world's biggest overseas investors by 2020, June 25, 2011.

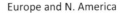

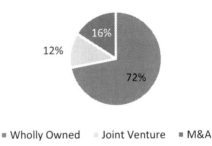

Figure 4:   Market Entry Mode: Europe and North America
Source: Wen and Liyun (2015, p. 149).

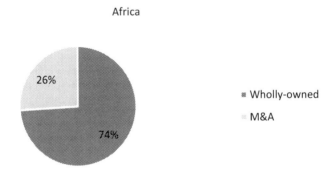

Figure 5:   Market Entry Mode: Africa
Source: Wen and Liyun (2015, p. 149).

to control capital outflows and 'irrational investments'.[7] The narrative on that investment remains complex and subject to biases, as summarised by Mark Halle of the International Institute for Sustainable Development (IISD)[8]:

> The discussion around China's foreign investment has been somewhat poisoned by, on the one hand, scaremongering by non-Chinese

---

[7]*Financial Times*, State-led companies back on top in China's outbound M&A rankings, September 3, 2017.
[8]*IISD*, What China's overseas investment means for the rest of the world, February 2016.

commentators, and on the other by an overly defensive reaction by the Chinese to legitimate criticisms.

Part of that criticism, which many Western firms will attest to, is based on the view that Chinese buyers are unreliable. Some $230 billion of deals worth $1 billion or more have collapsed since 2012 because the Chinese buyers got cold feet at the last minute, failed to win government support, or withdrew because of a hostile reaction from authorities in the countries in which the targeted investments were domiciled.[9] This sense of complexity and uncertainty in dealing with Chinese firms adds to the fundamental biases against China.

---

[9] *The Economist,* Crossing the river, June 10, 2017, p. 61.

3

The Five Biases

Some people think that dogs and wolves look alike, but a dog knows a wolf when he sees it.

Anonymous

The internationalisation of Chinese firms presents some complicated management hazards beyond those normally associated with the liabilities of foreignness-facing firms expanding into international markets. For Chinese firms, these hazards reflect unconscious and conscious Western conformation biases — the propensity to interpret evidence as proof of the validity of views already held.

First Bias

The first bias combines the preferred modality of Chinese firms entering new markets, which is to increasingly acquire foreign-based businesses rather than enter through a joint-venture or take a risk on a Greenfield investment as well as the opaque and highly idiosyncratic nature of corporate governance in many Chinese firms.

In 2016, Chinese firms became the major force in cross-border M&A, accounting for $227 billion in transactions (not all completed), double the amount in 2015.[1] This preference for M&A has attracted attention from the international media, business, political, and scholarly community, many of whom attempt to frame this development in geopolitical and populist terms. In 2016, some $40 billion worth of acquisitions of Western firms by Chinese firms were blocked by governments,[2] with the US Committee on Foreign Investments in the United States (CFIUS) and the Australian Foreign Investment Review Board (FIRB) applying particularly scrutiny, due to a portrayal of fears of China as a security threat. Other deals have failed despite the Chinese buyer having offered a higher price, such as HNA's bid to buy the City Airport in London. HNA also found its attempts to buy New Zealand's largest finance company, UDC Finance, blocked by the New Zealand authorities because it could not be verified who controlled HNA.[3] When CNOOC, a Chinese oil company, tried to buy Unocal, a Californian energy business, there was a political outcry in the US, and the deal was blocked. When Huawei tried to acquire 3Com, a small US telecom company, that deal was blocked, as the media saw it as a threat to 'US national security'. In Australia, the attempt by Chinese mining company Chinalco to acquire an 18% stake in Rio Tinto for an estimated A$19.5 billion met significant political and media hostility *(members of the CCP would be sitting on the Rio board)* before the bid was eventually withdrawn. Also in Australia, Huawei was banned — on security grounds — from supplying aspects of the National Broadband Network, and security reasons were also used to block a bid from Minmetals for OZ Minerals, and an A$7.5 billion bid for NSW Ausgrid from a consortium including the SOE, State Grid, was also blocked for vaguely stated 'national security' reasons. The Australian government also blocked the sale of pastoral company S. Kidman & Co to a Chinese buyer on national interest grounds, creating a sense that 'national security' or 'national interest' issues are a smokescreen and investment

---

[1] *Financial Times*, Final quarter of blockbuster deals boosts M&A activity, January 2, 2017.
[2] *Financial Times*, Nearly $40 billion in Chinese acquisitions pushed back by West, October 22, 2016.
[3] *Financial Times*, New Zealand blocks HNA takeover of ANZ unit, December 21, 2017, p. 16.

barrier used to disguise other reasons, which may include nationalism, populism, racism, and protectionism. Despite the absence of fact in many cases, the bias creates an unfriendly atmosphere and discrimination towards Chinese firms, as Professor Nolan (2012) notes:

> Western governments view China's national champion firms in a fundamentally different way from that in which they view companies from other Western countries with substantial state ownership.

In theory, the ownership of a firm in a market economy should be irrelevant; in practice, it can be controversial when Chinese firms are involved. In part, this happens because of the firms' sometimes opaque, diverse, and hybrid ownership structures involving central, provincial, city, county, and even town and village governments. Suspicion in the West arises because many firms, state-owned enterprises (SOEs), and privately-owned enterprises (POEs) are affiliated with the chinese communist party (CCP), and many entrepreneurs are CCP members. It would be wrong to assume that China's growing private business environment reflects free contracting among private agents, as in a market economy. POEs are vulnerable to the whims of the CCP and can easily get caught in political crossfire when they conduct their affairs in a way that is not agreeable to the party, as was evident in the crackdown on overseas investment in 2017.[4,5] In a party-state, the goals of the business community and the rule of law are subordinated to the CCP; in practice, the primacy of the CCP is unconstrained. This reality has become more apparent under President Xi. This rejuvenation of the Party was underlined by the head of the Central Commission on Discipline Inspection (CCDI) and close ally to President Xi, Wang Qishan, who said: 'there is no such thing as the separation between the party and the government'.[6] In uttering these words, Wang Qishan was contradicting Deng

---

[4] *Financial Times*, State-led companies back on top in China's outbound M&A rankings, September 3, 2017b.
[5] *Financial Times*, Chinese crackdown on dealmakers reflects Xi power, August 9, 2017.
[6] *The Economist*, Xi Jinping after five years, October 14, 2017, pp. 16–18.

Xiaoping, who in 1980 had called for a separation between the Party and government.

The emphasis on political connections can create a perception that there is little to differentiate POEs from SOEs. This ambiguity was highlighted in Wen and Liyun (2015), when they define POEs as (i) individual and private enterprises; (ii) township enterprises; (iii) private technology enterprises; (iv) joint-stock enterprises that are not state-controlled; (v) foreign-owned enterprises that are not state-controlled; or (vi) state-owned (or publicly owned) but privately-run enterprises. This is a very broad definition but symptomatic of the ambiguity that can often surround a POE in China. This has resulted in a view among many Western government agencies that there is very little real distinction between a POE and an SOE, as both are likely to do what the CCP tells them to do, including intelligence gathering for the government, as a former US director of national intelligence commented when highlighting that Chinese smartphone firms control a third of the market worldwide: 'This is not just about market share, this is about intelligence-gathering, since Chinese law allows and implicitly encourages their intelligence services to use any and all communications and IT equipment for intelligence collection'.[7]

There is no getting past the fact that Chinese firms are politicised, and opaque ownership structures in many large firms such as HNA adds to the complexity and the highly idiosyncratic nature of corporate governance. CCP cells are embedded within firms; all major firms have a Party Committee (every firm of more than 50 people has a Party Secretary), and the in-house CCP meeting often shadows board meetings and sometimes trumps board decisions. In theory, the Party Committee's role is to advise management on how they should manage in line with the CCP's political goals. HNA founder and Chairman Chen Feng, for example, was a delegate to the National Congress of the CCP. Regarding SOEs, the State-Owned Assets Supervision and Administration Commission (SASAC) declared that 'all major decisions of the company must be studied and suggested by the Party's Committee'.[8] A key assessment criterion

---

[7] *The Australian*, Trump worse than Watergate: Spy chief, June 8, 2017, p. 4.
[8] *Financial Times*, Chinese developer rejects in-house communist party committee, January 16, 2017c.

is the degree to which management proposals are consistent with promoting a 'harmonious society', a proclaimed political priority. In many firms, the CCP secretary will hold one of the top roles. Thus, the principal–agent distinction can be blurred as 'mandarins and managers merge, the captains of industry are simultaneously cadres of the CCP-state' (Tang and Ward, 2003). The influence of the CCP highlights a dual-track corporate governance structure, with a board of directors in practice subject to the prerogative of executives or agents appointed by the CCP through the SASAC. To many in the West, the idiosyncratic nature of Chinese corporate governance is, to paraphrase Winston Churchill, like a 'riddle wrapped in a mystery inside an enigma'. Western anxiety reflects a belief that strategic decisions are likely to be influenced by CCP objectives and that, in the event of a conflict of interest between, say, conventional business practice and state objectives, the CCP will carry the day. In his excellent book *The Party* (2012), Richard McGregor points out that the chairmen of China's leading SOEs all have a 'red machine' sitting on their desks that provides an instant link to the CCP high command, and Halper (2010) describes the prevalence of tight links between the ruling elite and company bosses.

CCP membership amongst entrepreneurs built momentum from 2001 when President Jiang Zemin declared that the CCP should reflect a broader majority of Chinese society in what became known as the *Three Represents*. For entrepreneurs, a decision to be one of the close to 90 million members (6.5% of the population) of the CCP[9] is a rational choice with commercial benefits, including access to loans, managing regulatory conditions, and other factors that increase the value of the firm. There are many 'red hat' firms, whose underlying control resides with private owners but that for political network reasons are registered as SOEs. This reflects a perception that SOEs are treated like 'favourite sons' while POEs are 'the ugly stepson or stepdaughter'. Chinese POEs also rely on political connections to compensate for weak legal and formal institutional arrangements and to avoid the unwanted interference of CCP officials — particularly in

---

[9]The CCP has fewer members than Christian denominations in China which is estimated at 100 million members.

local government and particularly the 'dukes'[10] — in their business affairs. The problems faced by POEs are illustrated by the fact that only 53% of court rulings involving domestic firms are enforced (Nee and Opper, 2012). The rule of law is often applied with 'one eye open and one eye closed' depending on the circumstances and the status and connections of the alleged offender. The pivotal power of the dukes in their own jurisdictions and in the promotion of their economic interests and local policy agenda over central government objectives is not to be underestimated: *The mountains are high and the emperor is far away* (*shan gao, Huangdi yuan*).

Conflicts between the goals of the firm and the requirements of the CCP occur at both national and local levels. The expression *gong-gong shao le, po-po hai hen duo* ('fewer fathers-in-law, still too many mothers-in-law') sums up the relationship many firms have with governments and their agencies at all levels. Just when the central government (father-in-law) has provided more freedom, local governments and regulators (mother-in-law) can make life more challenging. Again, principal–agent problems arise — how owners make sure managers do what the owners expect and act as sound stewards of the owners' property and wealth — which has been evident in many corruption cases, particularly under President Xi's 'catching the tigers and flies' and 'killing the chicken to scare the monkeys' anti-corruption campaigns. Seeking to build business empires to advance managers' personal wealth is not unique to China and many leaders of China's SOE's have succumbed to the temptations that unchecked power and poor corporate governance can create. Western readers do not need this writer to list examples of the same issues documented in the West. Indeed, the West has provided a good 'how to' manual about it.

Despite the reforms in the 1990s aimed at reducing the number of SOEs (*grasp the large, let go of the small*), there are still some 150,000 of them (300,000 in 2005), two-thirds of which are owned by local gov-

---

[10] Powerful provincial leaders are often known as 'dukes' reflecting the historical title given to local leaders during Imperial times.

ernments and the rest under central control, overseen by the SASAC, with approximately 115 of the larger and strategically important SOEs supervised directly within the CCP hierarchy. The CEOs of these major SOEs are selected by the Central Organisation Department of the CCP, and it is common for individuals to move from roles in the political system into senior business roles and vice versa. The CCP maintains tight control over personnel issues within SOEs, and as noted earlier, the CCP Secretary within an SOE has significant power. It is no surprise that the major SOE bosses, with their connections in the political system, remain significant obstacles to any reform that would threaten their power and privileges. As former US Treasury Secretary Paulson (2015) notes, the key to success in any modern business is to pick a strong and commercially minded CEO, yet SOE CEO and senior management appointments are at the behest of the CCP and can operate in ways that are not easily reconciled with conventional business practice: 'In 2004, the CCP required the chairmen of China's three leading telecom companies to swap jobs as easily as if they were playing musical chairs...In 2011, Fu Chengyu, the executive running CNOOC, one evening received a phone call informing him that he was to report the next morning at Sinopec as its new chairman (Paulson, 2015)'. The same happened at the three biggest airlines in 2009 and at the three biggest oil companies in 2010. There is no doubt that the selection of senior appointments within SOEs does not lend itself to conventional commercial practice as understood in the West.

Under President Xi, despite claims that the SOE sector is to be reformed and that market discipline will play a greater role, the evidence is that the major SOEs are strengthening their grip on their industrial sectors despite poor productivity and costs to the economy that the IMF estimates at over \$1 trillion over the next decade. The priority is on making sure that the SOEs support the government's macroeconomic and industrial policies. In squashing any suggestion of depoliticising SOEs, President Xi went on record as saying, 'The party's leadership of SOEs is a major political principle, and that principle must be insisted on'.[11] Whilst there is little

---

[11] *The Economist*, China Inc., July 22, 2017, p. 55.

appetite for adopting a Singapore model for SOEs — based on holding companies such as those under Singaporean wealth fund Temasek — some evidence of reform is evident in the trend for distinguishing between SOEs that are commercial, or more like private firms, and those that are more like public service firms, such as Shanghai Metro. The former are being encouraged to operate more like private firms in how they hire and reward management.

Western commentators often criticise SOEs for being protected by the state despite their poor performance. However, protecting local firms and industries from competition has many precedents in the West, as does the visible hand of state-led industrial policy. Many Western countries promoted 'national champions', allowing state-owned firms to build scale and market power before eventually privatising them. This is particularly true for airline, energy, and telecommunication companies, as well as commercial banks. Australian examples include Qantas, Telstra, and the Commonwealth Bank of Australia (CBA). These firms arguably owe their market position to the legacy of state ownership, protection, or an accommodating government approach to in-market M&A, which concentrates power and reduces competition. In the 19th century, the US achieved rapid industrialisation due in part to tariffs and protectionist barriers that shielded the industries, which it maintained for over a 100 years. US industry also benefited from military expenditure that helped develop radio, satellites, and the Internet. The reality is that US economic history is far more complex and state supported than popular capitalist ideology would portray. (Srinivasan, 2017). Professor Nolan (2014) notes this phenomenon:

> Only if high-income countries' governments fully recognise the unequal nature of the global playing field of industrial competition and acknowledge the role that industrial policy played in their own catch-up in the past, can they appreciate the intensity of effort being made by some developing countries to enable their indigenous firms to catch-up with firms from high-income countries that dominate global markets.... a large fraction of the world's leading firms were supported in one way or another by their national government at some stage in their development.

What we see in China in terms of business practice and closeness to government reflects China's experience as a young market economy and is not dissimilar from the experience in the US economy in the 19th and early 20th centuries — or even today.

Does the West Represent a Role Model?

Rampant corruption is a blemish on China's reputation, which I discuss in Chapter 4. There are, of course, numerous examples of corruption in the West (e.g. Enron, Tyco, Arthur Andersen, Parmalat, WorldCom, VW, and RBS) together with excessive CEO compensation, even in firms that fail, as illustrated in the multi-million dollar sums paid to Fred Goodwin at RBS and Richard Fuld at Lehman Bros., which represented the worst examples of corruption and abuse.[12] There are also Western examples, including in Australia, of classic principal–agent problems, where CEO compensation is set at extraordinary high levels even though the firms under their stewardship have failed shareholders and other stakeholders, in some cases materially damaging the firm's reputation and medium-term prospects through poor investments and allowing damaging cultures to flourish. This rent-seeking behaviour by CEOs is highlighted by the fact that, in the 1980s, the CEOs of the 100 largest public firms earned 25 times more than their average worker. In 2016, they earned 130 times more.[13] Their high salaries can be further padded by a range of pension and retention incentives, often rarely linked to performance in a way that is not subject to gaming — from 2006 to 2014 nearly all of the 1,000 largest US firms by market capitalisation completely changed their CEO incentive metrics at least once, and almost 60% changed them more than once.[14] In many cases when the going gets tough, there is comfort in knowing that, if one is fired, significant rewards will crystallise in

---

[12] Richard Fuld, CEO, Lehman Bros., was paid $484 million in the period 2000–2007 prior to Lehman's filing for bankruptcy (*Forbes*, March 2012).

[13] *The Economist*, The Marxist Moment, May 13, 2017, p. 48.

[14] *Harvard Business Review*, Comp Targets That Work, September–October 2017, p. 104.

the form of termination payments and lucrative pension rights. This behaviour and weak corporate governance can extend to the not-for-profit sector, as became evident in 2017 with the A$4.9 million termination payment made to the CEO of Certified Practicing Accountant (CPA) in Australia. During the CEO's stewardship of the CPA, he allowed it to become embroiled in reputationally damaging conduct, including financing his self-promotion campaigns and failing basic tests of disclosure on senior executive remuneration. Rather than being fired without compensation for a failure of stewardship, as would happen in China, a passive board allegedly stacked with the CEO's friends and supporters, thought the solution was offering the CEO an excessive level of termination compensation. SOE bosses are at the other end of the spectrum. The CEO of PetroChina, China's largest oil company, earned 774,000 yuan ($112,000) in 2016; the CEO of US Chevron, with roughly the same market value, was paid $24.7 million.[15] Remuneration at the top Chinese SOEs would barely register in the middle-management ranks of the clear majority of Western top-100 firms within their own domestic markets.

The justification for CEO excesses is the proposition that firms have to hire in the global market for talent, even though most CEO appointments are company men (and very rarely women) who have worked their way through the ranks, many of whom had little prospect of an equivalent role as a free agent. This problem with aspects of capitalism, evident in many markets, is what Karl Marx had in mind when he argued that the capitalist class did not consist of wealth creators but of rent seekers, who are skilled, often aided by concentrated industry structures, at expropriating the efforts of others and who are helped by political agents to protect industry structures lacking in meaningful competition.

The modern history of the banking sectors in the UK, Australia, and the US are illustrative of some poor ethical conduct, rent-seeking behaviour, and weak corporate governance at a cost to customers and junior level employees, but which have ultimately rewarded senior executives

---

[15] *The Economist*, China Inc., July 22, 2017, p. 56.

and very rarely led to punishment. When Fred Goodwin was fired as CEO of RBS after the collapse and nationalisation of the bank, he left with a pension entitlement of $550,000 pa and a departing bonus of $7 million, whilst investors lost all their capital and thousands of employees lost their jobs. The example of JP Morgan is also illustrative. In 2016, US regulators accepted a $264 million settlement offer from JP Morgan, which admitted running a sophisticated jobs-for-mandates scheme, where children of senior Chinese officials were given jobs on the understanding that mandates would then be awarded to the bank by grateful parents. The JP Morgan 'Sons & Daughters' programme resulted in over 100 hires on behalf of Chinese officials at more than 20 SOEs and 10 government agencies. Some of the hires were so incompetent that they were referred to within JP Morgan as 'photocopiers'. The irony in these examples is that a Chinese official caught acting in a corrupt manner is likely to spend much of the remainder of his life in jail, whilst an employee of a Western institution can look to his employer to pay the fine at a cost to shareholders. Famously, in 2016, a whistle-blower at Deutsche Bank, Eric Ben-Artzi, refused his $8.5 million reward from the US Securities and Exchange Commission (SEC) on principle because he felt it was wrong that shareholders and employees who had lost their jobs should bear the cost when the responsible senior management went unpunished. The *Financial Times*[16] summarised the corporate governance agency problems in the West regarding Enron (with a summation that would still hold today regarding, for example, the collapse of Australian retailer Dick Smith in 2016, the scandal at the CPA in 2017 and the conduct issues that engulfed Australian banks in 2018)[17]:

> At the heart of the Enron scandal is a failure of corporate governance…an audit committee that signed misleading accounts. A Board that was ineffective in supervising senior management's actions. These failures are all too common…they exist, too, in companies where there are no scandals, merely poor performance or entrenched mediocrity.

---

[16] *Financial Times*, Failures of governance, February 12, 2002, p. 14.

[17] *Financial Times*, How an Australian bank laundered money for Hong Kong drug gangs, March 14, 2018, p. 27.

Critics of the close relationship between the CCP and the SOEs should also remember that, in the West, powerful industry groups such as the agricultural sector in the US (which receives up to $30 billion of taxpayer subsidies per annum) or the subsidies and protection extended to the banking sector in major economies such as the US, the UK, and Australia are all at the expense of the taxpayer and customers. The major banks in Australia, who are heavily concentrated in residential mortgage lending with household debt at eye-watering levels, benefit from an implicit 'too big to fail' government guarantee; essentially making the banks quasi-nationalised firms. In many ways, these essentially government-guaranteed privately-owned firms highlight growing societal angst concerning aspects of capitalism, whereby the risk of failure is covered by the taxpayer, but the rewards of success flow to shareholders and senior executives. The austerity measures that have plagued the UK economy following the GFC and the rewards that flowed to the RBS CEO and other bank executives highlight the asymmetry of the economic equation in many sectors of Western economies and help explain why many have lost trust in 'big business', banking in particular, and globalisation and capitalism more broadly, as developments that have enriched only the elite, often in ways that disadvantaged the many. Western governments cannot argue that their financial systems are free from government influence: the residential mortgage market in the US, for example, has government agencies accepting the risk on some 65–80% of all new home loans, with an estimated taxpayer subsidy for housing debt at $150 billion pa.[18] One newspaper summarised this paradox as follows: 'The biggest market in the US, real estate, makes a mockery of the country's reputation as a bastion of free enterprise. The level of government interference in the $26 trillion US housing market, continues to rise automatically with little scrutiny.'[19] The decision in 2009 by President Obama's administration to write off 90% of the debt held by General Motors shows how governments and

---

[18] *The Economist*, Comradely capitalism, August 20, 2016, pp. 15–17.
[19] *The Australian*, Land of the free and home of Fannie, Freddie, and Ginnie, September 10, 2016, p. 21.

big business in the West can be closely linked. That powerful industry groups carry much influence in many democracies is illustrated by the gambling business in Australia. Australia's gambling industry is amongst the biggest in the world, with estimated gambling losses (spending on gambling minus the pay-outs) of A$18.3 billion, close to $1,000 per adult in 2016.[20] In 2010, a government advisory board estimated that the social costs of gambling were A$4.7 billion a year and characterised slot machines (or 'pokies') as 'electronic cocaine'. These costs are likely to be materially understated given the human costs of an addiction that is skilfully manipulated among the most vulnerable. Despite this, local governments are reluctant to tamper with current practices, as they benefit from associated taxes to the tune of A$6 billion a year (despite the anti-social nature of pokies and the strong family ethos of sporting codes such as Australian Football League (AFL), they have become material contributors to the finances of the majority of AFL clubs, accounting for up to a third of all club revenues, with fans having lost in excess of $100 million in 2016 alone). The gaming industry also 'donates lavishly to both big political parties and to independent politicians', which prompted independent MP Andrew Wilkie to argue that such a practice 'corrupts governance and is no different from a bribe'.

Double-standards in the West are evident in the magnitude of corrosive donations to political parties by big business, for which the finance sector in Anglo-Saxon economies are well known. Donations by Chinese interests to political parties in countries such as Australia (where the major political parties received around A$6 million from Chinese sources between 2013 and 2015)[21] hardly present China with a model to emulate. Poor corporate governance and business and political rent seeking is alive in China, as it is in most Western economies. The so-called advantages that the West claims to have in this area do not stand up to scrutiny.

---

[20] *The Economist*, The biggest losers, March 18, 2017, p. 22. *Herald Sun*, AFL pokies shame, April 16, 2017, p. 7.

[21] *The Australian*, Beware soft power influences bearing gifts, September 3, 2016, p. 18.

Second Bias

A second bias is the popular perception that, with the invisible hand of the CCP and foreign exchange reserves of approximately $3 trillion, China is buying the world, engaging in a protracted strategy game of *Wei qi* (a popular Chinese board game of surrounding pieces) that can be interpreted as a strategy of encirclement. This theory is reinforced by the view that China is awash in cheap capital that is fuelling a global shopping spree, as with the Japanese firms in the 1980s.

Linked to this theory is the view that an economic Cold War could eventuate between China's unique form of state capitalism and the more *laissez-faire* capitalism in the West. This reaction is in part linked to the rapid rise of China and the aspirations that President Xi has for the 'China Dream' (which some in the West see as opposing the American dream) and is evident in many initiatives such as the One Belt, One Road (OBOR) project, which I discuss in Chapter 4. Western anxiety can also be found in regular media commentary and in books such as *The Hundred-Year Marathon, China's Secret Strategy to Replace America as the Global Superpower* (Pillsbury, 2016), *Will China Dominate the 21st Century?* (Fenby, 2014), *When China Rules The World: The Rise of the Middle Kingdom and the End of the Western World* (Jacques, 2009), *The Beijing Consensus: How China's Authoritarian Model Will Dominate the Twenty-First Century* (Halper, 2010), *A Contest for Supremacy: China, America, and the Struggle for Mastery in Asia* (Friedberg, 2011); *Eclipse: Living in the Shadow of China's Economic Dominance* (Subramaniam, 2011); *China versus the West: The Global Power Shift of the 21st Century* (Tselichtchev, 2012); *China's Silent Army: The Pioneers, Traders, Fixers and Workers Who Are Remaking the World in Beijing's Image* (Cardenal and Araujo, 2013), and *By All Means Necessary — How China's Resource Quest is Changing the World* (Economy and Levi, 2015).

These and other commentators link the rise of Chinese firms in the international economy with the threat to the hegemonic power of the US even though China was never a missionary society seeking to convert others to their values in the way that many Western powers have been and are. Just as the 20th century was marked by

American exceptionalism, the 19th century was marked by British exceptionalism. Sceptics point to the warning from highly respected Singaporean leader Lee Kuan Yew, who stated, 'It is China's intention to be the greatest power in the world'.[22] As I discuss in Chapter 4, the anxiety in the US and the West generally is that, for the first time in modern history, there is a competing ideology that will soon be the largest economy in the world and a state that does not want to belong to the US-designed international system. This anxiety is, however, not dissimilar to that about the economic power of the Japanese in the 1980s and crowds out a more measured assessment of China's international intent.

As discussed in Chapters 1 and 2, whilst Chinese firms have been rapidly expanding internationally in a relatively short period, the world's markets continue to be overwhelmingly dominated by Western and some Asian (Japanese and South Korean) multinationals. Professor Nolan (2012) described these firms as 'system integrators' with long histories, often involving M&A, dominant brands, superior technologies, large R&D investments, tremendous capacity for innovation, and the ability to attract the best international talent, together with a track record in developing such talent. The real scope of many of these firms extends way beyond their legal entity, consistent with Nolan's 'systems integrator' description. *The Economist* noted that[23]

> Big companies have reaped enormous efficiencies by creating supply chains that stretch around the world and involve hundreds of partners, ranging from wholly owned subsidiaries to outside contractors … They are forming ever more complicated alliances … Americas top 1,000 public companies now derive 40% of their revenue from alliances, compared with just 1% in 1980.

These Western firms exert strong control over their value chain and seek to serve the needs of the global middle class, with a long history in international business and a deeply developed knowledge

---

[22] *Forbes*, China's growing might and the consequences, March 9, 2011.
[23] *The Economist*, The rise of the superstar, September 17, 2016.

of managing cross-cultural and stakeholder dynamics. They strongly exhibit all the attributes of the Four Cs framework and source much of their management talent from leading Western business schools.

What is an International Firm?

When we talk about international firms, it is important to be able to measure just how international a firm's activities are. In the context of a firms' entire operations, having a small international presence would hardly qualify a firm as an international business. Many Western firms have a large international presence, and many more have relatively modest operations outside their domestic market. One simple, albeit imperfect, way to measure the internationalisation of a firm is to use the Trans-Nationality Index (TNI).[24] The TNI formula calculated as the arithmetic mean is

$$TNI = (FSTS + FETE + FATA)/3,$$

where Foreign Share in Total Sales (FSTS), which is the ratio of overseas sales to total sales;

Foreign Employment in Total Employment (FETE), which is foreign employees as a percentage of total employees;

Foreign Assets in Total Assets (FATA), which is the ratio of overseas assets to total firm assets.

A high TNI (>50%) would *prima facie* denote a true international firm, although there is no measure for the size of a firm's home country market, the diversification of its international activities, or the fact that a new wave of technology-based global firms are often asset and people-light. These and other imperfections aside, on the TNI measure, firms from the US, Japan, and Europe (principally Germany and the UK) dominate, as do firms from the pharmaceutical, motor vehicles, telecommunications, electronics, and oil and gas industries. Chinese firms, whilst prevalent in the *Fortune* and *FT 500* indices, are

---

[24] The TNI was developed by the United Nations Conference on Trade and Development (UNCTAD).

not yet among the top 500 firms as measured by the TNI. This is illustrated by the Chinese banks, which feature prominently in the league tables of the world's largest banks, yet the scope of their international operations barely registers compared to the world's leading banks such as JP Morgan, Citibank, HSBC, or Standard Chartered. China does not have a single bank that is globally competitive.

Western firms still have national characteristics and remain rooted in their dominant national cultures, which shape how they behave and how they might be influenced — a reality starkly highlighted by the promises of US President Trump to impose costs on firms that take their operations outside the US and by the decision of the Ford Motor Company to cancel, after President Trump's election, plans to invest $1.6 billion in a new plant in Mexico and instead invest in Michigan.[25] In comparing the relative strength of the system integrators, Professor Nolan (2012) describes as a myth any sense that China is buying the world, highlighting the irony that virtually all leading multinational firms operate inside China — albeit critical of the degrees of freedom and the lack of a level playing field — and are pushing to be given more scope to grow. Nolan's balanced analysis can be summarised as *the West is inside China, but China is not inside the West.* He suggests that technical expertise and cultural and political incompatibilities may form 'insurmountable challenges' for Chinese firms' international expansion. The concept of *hard* barriers, where investment requests are rejected on 'national interest' grounds, and *soft* barriers, where more passive measures and media rhetoric may be used to constrain the international growth of Chinese firms, represent a daunting reality. One example of media rhetoric and public perception being at odds with reality is the acquisitions of farm assets in Australia, where there is a popular perception that Chinese buyers are acquiring much of the available farmland. When the Australian government revealed its register[26] on foreign-owned

[25] *Financial Times*, Trump turns his ire on Toyota's car plant, January 5, 2017.
[26] *ABC News*, http://ab.co/2c15wON, 'UK tops list of foreign investments in Australian farmland; China owns 0.5 per cent', September 6, 2016.

farmland in 2016, it showed that 13.6% of farmland was owned by foreigners, with 53% of that portion owned by British, followed by the US, Dutch, and Singaporean investors; well down the list were Chinese investors, with 2.8% of foreign land ownership and less than 0.5% of total agricultural land across Australia. This is a classic case of the truth inconveniently being at odds with the rhetoric; in a world of populist media and a propensity for Internet-assisted misinformation ('fake news'), bias can remain undaunted by the facts.

KPMG/University of Sydney research from 2015 provides evidence of the liability of foreignness and the difficulty Chinese firms face integrating into Australia. The research[27] consisted of a mailed survey completed by 51 Australia-based Chinese firms (20 SOEs and 31 POEs) and highlights the problem of bias, evident in the negative media coverage, with only 16% of respondents agreeing that Australian media were supportive of Chinese investment despite the significant economic benefits it brought. The same survey highlights that Chinese firms feel discriminated against, with firms from other countries made to feel more welcome and enjoying better terms and conditions. A total of 50% of respondents felt Australians were more welcoming to investors from other countries, and 28% were neutral on the question. This is consistent with the discrimination bias hypothesis regarding Chinese firms operating in international markets.

Third Bias

A third bias relates to the perceived quality of Chinese products and the lack of international brand ownership. Many in the West view 'quality' and 'Made in China' as a contradiction in terms and claim that the best advice to anyone buying Chinese-made good is 'caveat emptor' ('buyer beware'). Moving away from being low-cost manufacturers and assemblers to the world to having a stronger brand identity in international markets is a goal of many Chinese firms such as

---

[27] See www.kpmg.com.au and demystifyingchina.com.au. December 2015. See also Appendix 3.

Alibaba, Xiaomi, Haier, Fosun, Goodbaby, HNA, Anbang, and Huawei. The desire to create and build global brands is logical, as the economics of brand ownership are much more attractive than that of low-cost manufacturing. Whilst Chinese firms play an important role in the global supply chain of many global brands, the example of iPhone is illustrative of the weak economics of brawn over brain and plays to the view that China is a labour–cost arbitrage player in the global value chain. iPhones are assembled in China, but less than 5% of its value is captured there. The vast bulk of its value is captured by the brand in the US; look on the back of any iPhone and you will read 'Designed by Apple in California…Assembled in China'. Contrary to the myth that Chinese firms are swamping the world with low-cost and low-quality technology products, over 80% of China's high-tech exports are made by foreign-owned firms. The myth of China as a low value-added manufacturer was dispelled in a study by Britain's University of Sussex for the European Commission, which concluded that the iPhone example 'is far from representative'. The researchers calculate that the average value China adds to its exports is 76% (the EU's is 87%). The World Bank reaches similar conclusions.[28]

China has not been a noticeable developer or owner of global brands, despite the growth in OFDI. In brand management, reputation can be critical to success, and reputations can be based on perceptions, which are very important in global markets because that is often all that consumers have to go by. Reputation for Chinese firms has been mixed, with a generally negative connotation associated with 'Made in China', as described critically in Jeremy Haft's *Unmade in China* (2015). In another book, Midler (2011) describes how Chinese firms seek to grow margins by using inferior inputs, citing examples of toxic lead toys, drug-contaminated seafood, poisoned milk, poisoned pet food, toothpaste with industrial solvents, and unsafe steel and tyres, all adding to a perception that 'Made in China' is not a certification of quality in the way that 'Made in Germany' or 'Made in Japan' is. This reputation is damaging to China's national brand equity and Chinese firms.

---

[28] *The Economist*, The jewel in the crown, April 8, 2017.

There is no denying that China has had well-publicised quality problems. The reality is that Chinese firms can expect to be subject to competitor and nationalistic campaigns that feed consumer biases about the quality of Chinese products, crowding out facts and tarnishing 'brand China'. In the US, there is even a 'Throw It Out the Window' website about Chinese products.

The media play a big role, and tend to emphasise poor quality and safety issues, thus fuelling the unconscious bias in consumer perceptions. Haft (2015) writes that 'The Made in China safety scandals cannot be blamed on a group of wrongdoers. They are endemic. China's entire system is to blame for these ongoing safety failures'. Media reporting on China lends significant weight to negative news over positive news. An example of negative bias getting in the way of facts concerns China's weak reputation for product quality and safety, often related to toys (close to 90% of the world's toys are manufactured in China). However, as Beamish and Bapuji (2008) argue in their paper 'Toy Recalls and China: Emotion versus Evidence' based on research of toy recalls in the US between 1988 and 2007, 'the clear majority of recalls were due to flaws in product design, conducted in the corporate headquarters of toy companies, rather than poor manufacturing by factories in Asian countries'.

Does the West Represent a Role Model?

Product quality problems, incompetent management, corruption, and unethical management practices are, of course, not unique to China. Western examples include the horsemeat-in-beef scandal in Europe (2013), the VW emissions-cheating scandal (where the company sold 11 million cars using software deliberately designed to deceive the authorities about levels of environmentally damaging pollution (2015)), the BP oil spill in the Gulf of Mexico (2010), the Union Carbide pollution disaster in India (1984), the behaviour of many of the world's leading banks up to the GFC (2008), causing an economic crisis and misery in many developed economies, the collapse of accounting firm Arthur Andersen due to fraudulent practices (2002), the fraudulent practices at Enron (2001), fraudulent accounting at Worldcom (2002), the accounting scandal at Parmalat (2003), the theft of $600 million by the CEO and CFO of Tyco Industries in the US (2005), the bribery case against Siemens AG related to the bidding process for new hospitals in Jilin province (2006), the incompetence at RBS, the liabilities of which rose to $3.2 trillion when it was rescued by the British government (Britain's GDP at that time in 2009 was $2.6 trillion), the Bernie Madoff Ponzi scheme (2009) in the US involving $65 billion of client money, the corruption at FIFA (2015), the drug cheating scandal that engulfed AFL club Essendon (2015), the $400 million overstatement of profits by UK retailer Tesco (2014), the fake customer account scandal at Wells Fargo (2016), as discussed earlier, the $264 million payment made by JP Morgan (2016) to settle allegations under the Foreign Corrupt Practices Act that it hired children (all unqualified candidates for prestigious jobs[29]) of highly placed Chinese officials to gain business in China, the UK High Court ruling (2017) detailing systematic bribery and corruption at one of the world's leading brands, Rolls-Royce, between 1989 and 2003, and Samsung's lethal iPhone product deficiency (2016). The list goes on. Reputationally damaged firms in China pale into insignificance compared to what has occurred in the West. These examples all show that the problems about which China is criticised are prevalent in the West, despite its relative advantage in the strength and history of its institutions, including the rule of law. Before criticising China, many in the West should first take a good look in a full-length mirror and remember the advice of 'not throwing stones when living in a glass house'. China, as a developing nation, should be cut some slack.

Fourth Bias

A fourth bias, related to the third, is the view that China is a 'country of copycat firms', where weak property rights allow imitators to

---

[29] *The Financial Times* (November 19, 2016, p. 20) reported an internal JP Morgan email referring to one of the candidates 'as the worst candidate they have ever seen, and we must obviously had to extend him an offer'.

benefit from the innovation and risk-taking of Western firms. In 2014, then-US Vice President Joe Biden declared in a speech, 'I challenge you: name me one innovative product that has come out of China' (Tse, 2015). In both an article in the HBR entitled 'Why China Cannot Innovate' and in a book, Harvard academics Abrami *et al.* (2014) declared, 'The West is home to creative business thinkers and innovators, and China is largely a land of rule-bound rote learners — a place where R&D is diligently pursued but breakthroughs are rare'. Whilst it is true that the weak protection of intellectual property through the Chinese legal system is a risk to innovators and that many Chinese firms are plodders (as are many Western firms), these views play to a negative bias about Chinese firms and ignore the progress made in a relatively short period by firms such as Tencent, Xiaomis, Alibaba, JD.Com, Lenovo, and Haier and the innovation driven by firms in the $1.8 trillion fintech sector. Huawei, for example, spends more on R&D than Apple does and is one of the world's most prolific generators of high-quality international patents.[30]

The impressive growth of China's digital firms has been assisted by the lack of legacy infrastructure, particularly in retail and finance. The innovations from Tencent-owned mobile-messaging service WeChat, for example, outstrips the capabilities of Western competitors and leaves Chinese travellers to the West feeling that they are stepping back in time when they look at the mobile/Internet payment capabilities and an array of other services offered in the West. WeChat, first released in 2011, had 800 million users in China and several million elsewhere (some 1,500 Australian retailers have WeChat Pay at point of sale), is more akin to an entire ecommerce platform than a messaging app and has quickly become a trusted brand in China in the same way that Alibaba has, with many Western commentators believing that WeChat will come to define mobile Internet capabilities in the West. Alibaba, an ecommerce giant, pioneered the use of escrow in online payments, which built trust and made consumers confident about using online merchants through its affiliate Alipay. The volume of mobile payments in China reached

---

[30] *The Economist*, The jewel in the crown, April 8, 2017.

$8.6 trillion in 2016, compared to $112 billion in the US.[31] As the *Financial Times* reported, 'You can go for weeks in China without cash, swiping your phone to pay for coffees, clothing or utility bills. So ubiquitous is Alipay, its online payment platform, that even some rough sleepers accept donations via it'.[32] China's digital payment market is almost 50 times the size of that in the US,[33] and its founder, Jack Ma, internationally known and highly politically connected amongst world leaders, has plans for Alibaba to build its own NASA and a global trading platform for small and medium-sized firms, which Alibaba calls 'project e-WTO' in reference to the World Trade Organisation. Whilst China lags behind the US and many European markets in the quality of its shopping centres and physical shops selling branded goods, this has created an opportunity for WeChat and Alibaba to fill the gap with market-leading ecommerce solutions. In 2016, ecommerce retailing accounted for 18% of all sales in China compared to about 8% in the US.[34]

Anyone using the Shanghai metro would quickly see just how advanced some parts of China have become. The engaging smartphone screens provide customers with a variety of sources of functionality. The pace and scale of digitalisation of China is eye-opening. The bias in the West also ignores the contribution of ethnic Chinese foreign-invested firms, which Fuller (2016) describes as the 'hidden dragons driving Chinese technological development'. In their excellent book, Yip and McKern (2016) argue that technological disruptive business models are flourishing in China, where digitally sophisticated consumers are quick to adopt new trends, and that the old paradigm for the innovation capacity of Chinese firms is exactly that — old and out of date.

China is also well placed to lead the world in the development and application of electrical vehicles. Apart from the incentive to do

---

[31] *The Economist*, Innovation in China, September 23, 2017, p. 17.

[32] *The Financial Times*, Alibaba, May 25, 2017, p. 9.

[33] *The Financial Times*, China's digital economy is a global trailblazer, March 21, 2017, p. 18.

[34] *The Financial Times*, China's internet is flourishing inside the wall, November 24, 2016, p. 19.

something about the level of pollution choking many Chinese cities, and the reliance that the Chinese auto market — the largest in the world — has on oil imports, the Chinese authorities see the electric vehicle market as one where it can be a global leader. China is already the world's largest maker of electric vehicles, having sold 507,00 vehicles, 45% of the world's total, in 2016, with plans to manufacture 7 million vehicles by 2025.[35] The development of an electrical vehicle industry is an integral part of the 'Made in China 2025' strategy and following examples from state-sponsored industry promotion in other Asian markets such as South Korea and Japan, the Chinese authorities sees this strategy as a way of breaking the stranglehold a select group of developed nations have on the auto industry.

Another industry to watch is China's fledgling pharmaceutical firms, such as Shanghai-based biotech firm China-Med. Boosted by government support and an influx of foreign talent, China has the potential to become a leader in research and development given the cost advantage in developing new drugs in China relative to the US and Europe.[36] As discussed in Chapter 1, China has a history of innovations that have shaped the modern world. That tradition for innovation was allowed to lapse due to an isolationist policy and a sense of superiority that engulfed imperial China from 1500, as Lord Macartney's expedition discovered in 1793. The tragedy of the Century of Humiliation from 1839 and then the period of ideologically driven policy under Mao from 1949 to 1978 came at a great cost to the economic progress of China. Arguably, this negative bias towards Chinese firms has parallels to the 1980s, when the rise of Japanese firms in the international economy, supported by a cheap cost of capital, compliant banks, and soft budget targets, was viewed as a state-sponsored threat to the US. When a clear-minded assessment of Japanese firms was eventually made, it became evident that they were introducing a range of innovations to manufacturing and product quality. Their emphasis on quality control helped develop just-in-time manufacturing and six-sigma

---

[35] *The Financial Times*, China's highly charged power play, October 13, 2017, p. 9.

[36] *The Economist*, A better pill from China, March 18, 2017, p. 66.

disciplines, which were to revolutionise practices in many Western firms well beyond manufacturing.

Today, however, China is making startling progress. As *The Economist*[37] has noted that Shenzen alone debunks the outdated myth of 'copycat China' as it becomes a world-class cluster for innovation. In 2016, close to $80 billion of venture capital investment poured into Chinese firms, compared to $12 billion from 2011 to 2013.[38] Moreover, the government's commitment to R&D, currently at 2.1% of GDP, is growing though still lagging the 2.9% spent in the US, 3.3% in Japan, and 4.2% in South Korea. Impressive as these figures are, Professor David Shambaugh (2016) warns, this spending will not advance the innovation agenda to its full potential given the 'deeply ingrained rote memorisation and repetitive pedagogy in Chinese education… and the chronic intrinsic weaknesses of the Chinese education system', which I touch on in Chapter 8.

Fifth Bias

A fifth bias is that the Chinese economy is caught in four traps: aging demographics, a middle-income economy, misallocated and under-priced capital, and high levels of debt. Consequently, populist views suggest that China will experience an economic hard landing and that the CCP will lose its legitimacy with contagion effects for Chinese firms operating in international markets. China will, in other words, become a classic 'Black Swan' event in the sense described by Nassim Nicholas Taleb (2007). A 'black swan' is a highly improbable event with three principal characteristics: it is unpredictable; it carriers a massive impact; and, after the event, we rationalise an explanation that becomes self-evident and therefore should have been predictable — in this case, the economic collapse of China and the demise of the CCP. The belief that China faces this outcome is largely based on the view that the CCP and the economy are locked in a path-dependent future: changing the direction of

---

[37] *The Economist*, Jewel in the crown, April 8, 2017.
[38] *The Economist*, Innovation in China, September 23, 2017, p. 17.

the economy is too difficult and carries too much legitimacy risk for the CCP, so they are locked into a future direction that is a continuation of the historical path. In the words of Professor Minxin Pei (2006), China is caught in a 'trapped transition'.

Evidence of pressures on society and the economy can be found in China's growing urbanisation, which in 2015 was at 55.6% up from 17% in 1978, and the Gini coefficient — a measure of income distribution — which in 2015 was 0.46, compared to an OECD average of 0.32 (US 0.41, Germany 0.30, Japan 0.32, and Australia 0.34). The World Bank considers a Gini coefficient above 0.40 to represent severe income inequality. In the 1980s, China's coefficient was 0.3.[39] In a socialist society, a Gini coefficient should be closer to 0.[40] China's growing wealth gap is highlighted by the concentration of wealth in a new class of billionaires with the top 1% accounting for over 30% of wealth and the bottom 50% accounting for close to 5%. Up until the mid-1990s, China experienced 'reform without losers'. Today, the situation is very different (Figure 1).

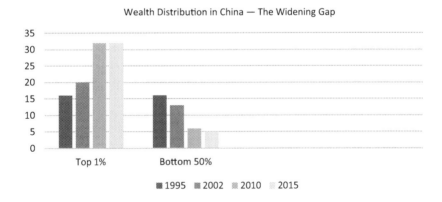

Figure 1:   Wealth Distribution in China

Source: Infographic, ABC News: China's growing wealth gap 1995–2015.

---

[39] *Financial Times*, China's income inequality among the world's worst, January 14, 2016.

[40] A Gini coefficient measures the income distribution within a country. The measure ranges from 0 to 1 and provides a guide between the rich and poor. 0 represents perfect equality, and 1 represents perfect inequality.

The significant gap in the concentration of wealth highlights the inadequacies of GDP growth as a measure of economic development, with China home to 400 million poor, with 25% of Chinese households accounting for only 1% of the country's wealth. There is a 'floating population' of internal migrants, mainly from rural areas, who lack the full entitlements of the household registration system (*hukou system*) with its access to public services, struggle to integrate into their new urban habitat, and form part of a 'hidden' unemployment. Studies have estimated that two-thirds of Chinese rural wives live apart from their husbands and that over 40 million children nationwide are left behind in rural areas while both parents work elsewhere.[41] The widening gap between urban and rural China is a major issue. China's major cities look like Europe while rural towns and villages like Africa (Zhang, 2011). Thus, whilst urbanisation has been a major factor in economic growth, a fact highlighted by University of Chicago economist and Nobel laureate Robert Fogel — who argued that the productivity of an industrial worker is five times that of an agricultural worker — some material social costs are not captured in GDP measures.

Much has been written about Japan's demographic challenge with an ageing population and low birth rate, but another looming challenge for China is the demographic clock, which because of the one child policy will see China soon face into a dependency ratio where the number of over 60 years old grows from 130 million in 2000 to 350 million by 2030 (Shirk, 2007). The dependency ratio compares those not in the labour force with those who are of working age (Age dependency = (people younger than 15 and older than 64/(working age people ages 15–64)). In 1987, 64% of the population were of working age and only 4.2% were aged 65 and above. The over 65's is now close to 14% and growing,[42] the UN estimates that the figure could rise to 45% by 2050. As Chinese scholar, Professor Barry Naughton (2006) commented: 'China will grow old before it has the opportunity to grow rich'. This is a problem which

---

[41] *JP Morgan*, Revitalising China through Reform, China Summit, June 3–5, 2013.
[42] *The Diplomat*, China's Struggle with Demographic Change, June 20, 2017.

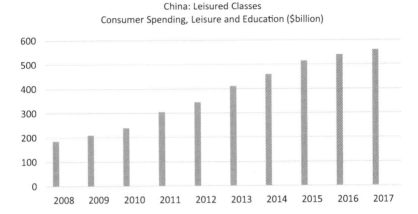

Figure 2:   Growing Middle-class Consumption Patterns

Source: The Economist, The World in 2017, p. 98.

has economic and societal implications, for which there are no quick fixes.

For areas of vulnerability that highlight the stark nature of inequality, critics point to the rising expectations of a growing Internet and social media-savvy and increasingly internationally aware middle class, which is forecasted to reach 275 million people by 2020, taking some 120 million overseas trips per annum, as they did in 2015. As Figure 2 illustrates, there has been a significant growth in 'middle-class' expenditures in China since 2008.

These and many other challenges facing China highlight the paradox of GDP growth, an incomplete measure of economic development, and the danger hidden in broad-based aggregates as a basis for understanding. GDP is a measure of output and does not measure inputs, thus ignoring important measures such as environmental costs, natural resource depletion, sustainability, and factor productivity. Noble Prize-winning economist Amartya Sen (1999) argued that economic development should also be assessed in terms of the opportunities and freedoms people enjoy, including the ability to escape poverty, enjoy healthcare, express political views, and seek higher education. On all these measures, China has much work to do. As I discuss in Chapter 4, however, the rise of populism in the West is partly a result of disillusionment with many aspects of

Western society, with inequality, unhappiness, narcissism, and anxiety rising to palpable levels.

Critics also warn of the imperfections in Chinese capital markets, particularly the underdeveloped and fragile bank-dominated financial system, which includes an opaque shadow-banking system that has been growing at 30% annually since 2012, and a high level of debt (including household debt), which has grown from 140% of GDP in 2008 to 260% at the end of 2016,[43] with some forecasting that it could reach close to 300% of GDP,[44] creating a mighty credit bubble (Figure 3).

Corporate liabilities, including the SOE sector, amounted to 166% of GDP at the end of 2016. The SOE sector, in particular, is highly indebted, with the IMF estimating that SOE debt-to-equity ratio rose from 1.3 in 2005 to 1.6 in 2014, whereas the average for POEs was below 0.8.[45] Equally concerning is that the productivity of capital in China has been declining. *The Economist* notes, 'it now

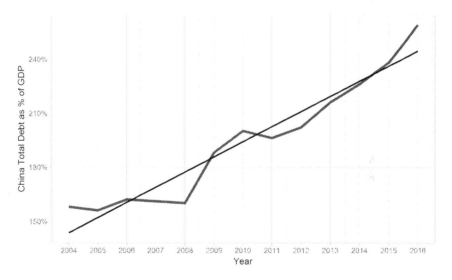

Figure 3:   Growth in Total Chinese Debt as % of GDP

Source: Bloomberg. Including corporate, household, government, and bank debt.

---

[43] *The Economist*, Special report on finance in China, May 7, 2016; see also *The Economist*, July 9, 2016, p. 62.

[44] *The Economist*, Smooth sailing, until it's not, December 24, 2016, pp. 14–15.

[45] *The Economist*, The world if, July 16, 2016, p. 10.

takes four yuan of new credit to generate one yuan of additional GDP, up from just over one yuan of credit before the global financial crisis'. The risk is that these conditions, which are unsustainable, will create a meltdown in the Chinese economy, with global contagion risk, impacting businesses and markets. Some evidence of this risk was outlined in *The Economist*,[46] which suggested that, despite relatively quarantined financial markets protected by capital controls, China's impact on Asian markets is now nearly as potent as is the US. The IMF estimates that the correlation between the Chinese stock market and those in other Asian markets is now 0.3 and rising (1 is a 'perfect' correlation), whereas the correlation between the stock market in the US and Asian markets is 0.4.

The nature of the risks in the Chinese economy are amplified (and best understood) by what economist Hyman Minsky called the 'financial-instability hypothesis', which argues that long periods of debt-fuelled prosperity sow the seeds of a looming financial crisis. This happens because excessive borrowing is invested in largely unproductive assets; eventually, there is day of reckoning, with severe economic consequences, as was evident during the GFC in 2008. The existence of this risk in the Chinese economy was acknowledged by the retiring governor of the People's Bank of China, Zhou Xiaochuan, who warned about complacency and the risks associated with excessive debt and speculative investment.[47] Evidencing this risk, McKinsey & Co. pointed out that the ratio of non-performing loans within the banking system in 2015 was closer to a crippling 7% than the officially reported 1.7%.[48]

Does the West Represent a Role Model?

The criticism of the weaknesses and risks within the Chinese financial system and thus the vulnerability of many firms that, though already

---

[46] *The Economist*, Chinese sneezes — Financial contagion from China now rivals that from America, September 24, 2016, p. 68.

[47] *Financial Times*, China Bank governor talks bluntly as retirement looms, October 23, 2017.

[48] McKinsey Global Institute, *China's Choice: Capturing the $5 Trillion Productivity Opportunity*, June 2016.

highly indebted, have taken on more financial risk to acquire foreign businesses is legitimate. This is amplified by the 'lemon' risk of overpaying for poor-quality businesses in foreign markets, which is discussed in detail in Chapter 7. Critics in the West know from first-hand experience the follies of a reckless financial system, as was demonstrated by the GFC. Banks in the US, UK, and Europe that positioned themselves as 'masters of the universe' eager to teach the Chinese and others how to run banks and develop a deep and broad financial system now offer numerous case studies in poor, unethical, and sometimes reckless corporate governance and management, together with weak regulation. If it were not for the coordinated efforts of governments in most developed economies, many banks with long and proud histories would not have survived (Brown, 2010).

Even in apparently strong Western banking systems, the degree of underlying economic risk can be high due to, for example, an overconcentration in certain asset classes such as housing, particularly speculative housing investment — where an implicit government guarantee can underpin activity that history may eventually describe as imprudent if not reckless (the UK and Australian banking systems exhibit this risk). The Chinese banking system has some serious challenges, but the West is no longer a credible reference point for how to manage and regulate banks.

Putting aside the contradictions, these five biases add to the liabilities of foreignness-facing Chinese firms and are complex, as they combine conventional business issues with geopolitical considerations in a way that is arguably unique to Chinese firms. These are not discreet biases but form part of a web of perceptions in the West that are subject to confirmation bias and ultimately represent a form of discrimination. For Chinese firms, these five biases represent management challenges over and above the conventional hazards firms face in internationalising their business and thus place an even greater onus on the quality of management. Added to these arguably insurmountable biases is the substantial barrier of opposing political ideologies.

4

The Barrier of Political Ideology

May you live in interesting times.
Old Chinese Saying[1]

This chapter might feel to some readers like a digression for a book on international business, but the foundation of the conformation biases discussed in the previous chapter is the criticism and suspicion of Chinese firms based on a philosophical and ideological difficulty with communism and a society based on undemocratic values.

This suspicion is based on deeply held views in the West on the superiority of liberal democracies and the freedoms normally associated with these values and beliefs. Most people in the West from World War II onwards, throughout the rise of the US as a superpower and then the eventual collapse of the Soviet Union and communism in Eastern Europe between 1989 and 1991, came to accept like a religious truth that nations based on liberal democratic values are 'good' while those not based on these values are 'bad' or inferior. The near collapse of the global financial system during the Global Financial Crisis (GFC), which resulted in large-scale government (taxpayer) intervention to save the global economy

---

[1] There is some dispute as to whether the origin of this saying is Chinese, but it is commonly understood to originate from the old Chinese curse 'may *he* live in interesting times'.

from disastrous consequences, highlighted the imperfections of the capitalist model and the huge economic damage of unregulated activities as a result of *laissez-faire* economic policies. Until the GFC, the intellectual hegemony of liberal democracy and the supremacy of capitalism was a blind faith that caused the mind to immediately close and the shutter to come down when alternative or competing views were presented.

We in the West are led to believe that all people would cherish living in a democracy if they could. The counter view that many in China and elsewhere believe is that champions of universal liberal democracy are no more than a Trojan horse[2] for the expansion of Western ideology, particularly American exceptionalism.

In the public domain, the debate has always been clouded by a sense that there are two states in the world — the liberal democratic state and the authoritarian state. In this polarised view, there are no shades of grey. Advocates for liberal democracy see open economies and open societies where universal freedoms are protected by the rule of law, sometimes embedded in a written constitution (so-called 'Washington consensus'). The Chinese Communist Party (CCP) disregards this theory: China's government values proletarian dicta-torship, authoritarian hierarchy and rule by the CCP rather than by law (so-called 'Beijing consensus'). The Chinese higher education sector is an example of where the two ideologies are in conflict. According to the 2015 CCP guidelines for higher education, lectur-ers are tasked with 'consolidating a common ideological basis for the united struggle of the entire Party, the entire country and all the people'. Critics of modern China dismiss the fact that it is less total-itarian and more capitalist, that the CCP has long committed itself to gradual, pragmatic, and experimental reform (consistent with Deng Xiaoping's philosophy of 'crossing the river by feeling for stones'), adopted the principles of a market economy for many but

---

[2]A 'Trojan horse' is a strategy where one party (the gifting party) causes another party to relax their security and allow activities that on the surface look innocent but disguise ulterior motives. The Trojan horse, rather than being innocuous, con-ceals significant risks and thus the true intentions of the gifting party.

not all sectors, enjoys growing social mobility as the household registration system (*hukou*) loosens, allows village-level elections in the countryside which potentially can be seen as part of an experiment with rudimentary democracy (though noting that villages are not units of government), and is progressively allowing greater freedoms as illustrated by what we are seeing as the fruits of a growing Chinese middle class. Professor Susan Shirk (2007) describe China as 'strong abroad but fragile at home'. Accepting this view, it is entirely rational for President Xi to use his first term to address foundation issues such as corruption and the rapid change within Chinese society — in a highly turbulent world — to seek to tighten the CCP's grip on society as necessary conditions before pushing for greater economic reform — a classic case of 'signalling left, before turning right'. The anti-China prejudice has only been reinforced by steps taken by President Xi to consolidate power and this at a time, as I discuss below, of unprecedented crisis with the legitimacy of democracy based on liberal values in many developed nations. The West has sought to portray President Xi as a 'new kind of Mao' (not since Deng Xiaoping, who like Mao, had ruled through the force of his personality and stature, has China evidenced a strong charismatic leader as is now evident in President Xi, who has established himself as China's paramount leader). Little regard is given by the critics to the fact that China is unique in its rich and complex history, the fresh memories of the Century of Humiliation, the deeply ingrained Confucian values, the sheer scale and scope of its land, which borders on 14 countries[3] (not all of them friendly or stable), the pace at which it is transforming, with close to 500 million people taken out of poverty since 1978, together with its status as a developing nation. The list goes on. Many commentators are unable to de-couple a progressive move in introducing values associated with a liberal democratic society and the need to retain a firm grip on political control, a recipe that worked so well in Singapore. The Chinese call this 'socialism with Chinese characteristics', or a

---

[3] Russia, India, Kazakhstan, Mongolia, Pakistan, Myanmar, Afghanistan, Vietnam, Laos, Kyrgyzstan, Nepal, Tajikistan, North Korea, and Bhutan.

'socialist market economy'. Haunted by lessons from the collapse of the Soviet Union, the CCP puts political stability ahead of all else; Professor Shirk notes that although never publicly articulated, the CCP's three dicta interconnected formula for stability are:

— Avoid public leadership splits
— Prevent large-scale social unrest
— Keep the military on the side of the party

Corruption

Inside China, the perception that corruption is endemic reinforces political cynicism and erodes popular support for the CCP. President Xi, in efforts led by his close ally, Wang Qishan, has prioritised a high-profile austerity and corruption campaign against rampant corruption and predatory behaviour by CCP officials, which distorts the economy and erodes the CCP's legitimacy. In a speech in 2014, President Xi described the challenge facing China:

> Corruption in regions and sectors is interwoven; cases of corruption through collusion are increasing; abuse of authority over personnel and abuse of executive authority overlap; the exchange of power for power; power for money, and power for sex is frequent; collusion between officials and businessmen and collusion between superiors and subordinates have become intertwined; the methods of transferring benefits to each other are concealed and various.[4]

President Xi's focus on corruption is not a new priority for a Chinese leader. President Hu Jintao portrayed himself as a leader willing to place his legacy on efforts to fight political corruption and clean up political life.[5] He vowed to wipe it out, but failed to do so. Under Xi's leadership there has been real and meaningful action.

---

[4] *Financial Times*, Too big, too Leninist — A China crisis is a matter of time, December 14, 2016.
[5] *China Daily*, July 1, 2006. See Shirk (2007: 32).

The CCP's Central Commission for Discipline Inspection (CCDI), which between 2012–2017 had begun disciplinary actions against 1.4 million party-members,[6] has placed great emphasis on catching the 'tigers' — government, military, and SOE officials with vice-ministerial rank or higher (between 2012 and 2017, 278,000 officials were punished, 440 at ministerial rank and above; 35 were members or alternates of the CCP's powerful Central Committee. That is as many as in all the years between 1949 and 2012).[7] Despite this crony capitalism remains endemic as so eloquently described by Professor Minxin Pie (2016) in his excellent book *China's Crony Capitalism: The Dynamics of Regime Decay*. He puts forward a theory — not exclusive to China — of 'collusion among elites', whereby the privatisation of SOEs is akin to looting by CCP insiders. The origins of modern corruption on the scale and of the nature now plaguing China can be traced back to Deng Xiaoping's tolerance for corruption as a response to the slow-moving bureaucracy that would have otherwise stifled the pace of much-needed reform. Whilst advocating punishment for serious abuses, Deng accepted that some local officials would bend the rules and get rich first, but that was an acceptable cost so long as they brought prosperity to their region: 'when you open the door, flies will get in' (Vogel, 2011). There is no arguing the fact that corruption in China has been assisted by ill-defined property rights, weak corporate governance, the decentralisation of administrative power — where the predatory dukes dictate policy and act in some regions as warlords in disguise — and the absence of institutional checks and balances and a scrutinising media. The challenges of rooting out corruption are partly systemic. Official salaries are modest, particularly relative to the power that many officials wield; thus, the incentive to accept illicit rewards is significant. Whilst it may be convenient to describe wide-scale corruption as a symptom or a trap of a developing economy in transition, where political and institutional reforms have not yet accompanied economic reform and political rent-seeking goes unchecked, the scale

---

[6] *The Economist*, Xi Jinping after 5 years, October 14, 2017, p. 17.
[7] www.bbc.com 'China's great purge under Xi', October 23, 2017.

of the current challenge may represent a danger to the legitimacy of the CCP.

Comparisons to India

Both China and India, the world's two most populous and geographically very large countries, achieved their independence in the late 1940s, and both started out as nations with broadly similar levels of economic development, but India as a democratic state and China a communist state. Almost 70 years later, the gap between these nations could not be wider. China's economy is three times that of India and its foreign trade almost four times larger; Chinese citizens, on average, live 10 years longer; and India's financial centre in Mumbai is a poor relation to Shanghai. In 2016, India and China both had a population of around 1.35 billion, but one had a GDP per capita of $8,438 (PPP: $17,050) and the other had equivalent figures of $1,772 (PPP: $7,110).[8] The gap between the two nations is growing wider, largely due to China's superior government and economic management, despite India being a democracy. Part of India's problem, *The Economist* reported, is that the coalition government lacks a majority in the upper chamber, undermining its ability to implement economic reform: 'the government's focus in the second half of its term will shift (away from reform) towards re-election'.

Crisis in the West

The lack of an open mind to the changes that have and are taking place in China comes at a time when there is a growing crisis of confidence with Western democracy. This is evident in the growing apathy and distrust for politics and politicians, as well as the growing tide of populist nationalism, which is increasingly looking like a populist uprising. When this shift in social attitudes took root is difficult to pinpoint, but political thinkers such as Francis Fukuyama[9] point to

---

[8] *The Economist*, The world in 2017, p. 98.

[9] Fukuyama, Francis, The coming collapse of America, *The Australian Financial Review*, December 28, 2016, pp. 22–27.

the GFC in 2008, which highlighted how capitalism had so dominated the economic and political agenda and how the economic elite had prospered by behaving with self-interest and sometimes recklessly, without accountability, leaving the cost of the resulting economic chaos to be paid by ordinary working- and middle-class citizens, who ultimately picked up the bill through austerity measures. There is much evidence of disquiet at the way wealth has been diverted away from lower- and middle-class workers, as evident in the growing trend of wages falling as a share of GDP. Figure 1 shows Australian wages dropping to just over 46% of GDP in 2016, the lowest figure since data collection began in 1959.

If a graph of corporate profits as a percentage of GDP was super-imposed over the top of labour costs, it would represent a mirror image, in reverse. Profits as a percentage of GDP are on track to break a new record in 2017–2018 and senior executive compensation, particularly CEO rewards likewise as they have become detached from any measure of sensibility or decency. Former Australian Treasurer, Peter Costello, in commenting on the major Australian banks, who

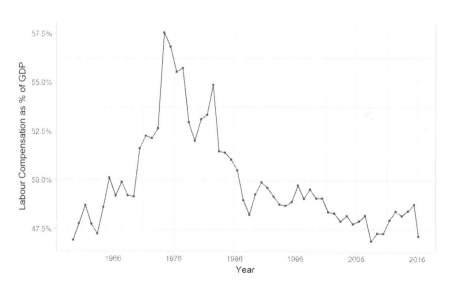

Figure 1: Australian Wages Relative to GDP

Source: ABS Catalogue 5206.0 — seasonally adjusted.

are amongst the most profitable in the world, said: 'they are absolutely immune from market discipline, living in a highly profitable cocoon; they think all these high returns are from their own brilliance, but what they haven't understood is they have a unique and privileged regulatory system which has delivered this to them'.[10] The broader story in the US and Europe is similar.[11] The flow-on effect has been the highest concentration of wealth since the 1920s.

The fallout from the GFC caused people to re-evaluate the limits of markets and question whether unbridled markets are the best societal approach to dealing with financial stability and the risk that herding will create asset bubbles, or dealing with environmental issues, where there is no profit motivation to act in the long-term interests of a sustainable environment. The political dynamics of the coal industry in Australia illustrative of this. Markets also reveal weaknesses in dealing with the provision of public goods, where there is limited incentives to generate profit. Markets also are poorly placed to deal with (in fact, have created) the excessive inequalities that plague many developed nations, as Fukuyama highlights. The reality, as argued eloquently by Professor Paul de Grauwe (2017), is a need for greater government involvement in dealing with many of the problems created by unrestrained or even poorly regulated markets.

Critics of China regularly point to the strong arm of the CCP intruding on the lives of its citizens through mechanisms such as plans for a 'social-credit system', which will score the behaviour of individuals according to 'creditworthiness' (which is also done in the West), social, and potentially political behaviour. In China, the national security law and the cyber security law give the CCP unrestricted access to all personal data, including data held by Alibaba, Baidu (China's largest search engine) and Tencent, which owns WeChat. These developments are an extreme version of the intrusion

---

[10] *The Australian*, Peter Costello's blast at the banks: Bring in some competition, August 19, 2017.
[11] *ABC News*, The G20 failed our youth as globalisation, deregulation and technology alienates workers, July 10, 2017.

that many national security experts and other government agencies are proposing in the West (which all add to the fear of how Big Data will be accessed and used). Chinese authorities argue that access to this data will allow it to monitor social attitudes without the need for elections, clamp down on corruption, and thus restore trust in public institutions. If the proposed plans come to fruition, China would, as *The Economist* describes, create the world's 'first digital totalitarian state'.[12] Critics also point to the attempts by the CCP to monitor the Internet as part of its campaign to ensure social stability as evidence of a totalitarian state clamping down on freedom of speech and other civil liberties. According to Professor Anne-Marie Brady, a Chinese scholar, 'only Iran, North Korea and Saudi Arabia have comparable levels of internet censorship'.[13]

A counter to this criticism however is that, whilst the Internet has democratised access to information, it has not necessarily improved the quality of information or addressed its potentially harmful use. There is evidence, for example, that social media has been used to interfere with the democratic process in Western nations through the planting of misleading stories.[14] It is hard to argue against the view that there are many negatives to the Internet that add to the decline in moral values, the rise in domestic and sexual violence, the increase in national security risk and the degree to which misinformation can easily be disseminated, as I discuss below, and with populism (often in the form of nationalism) and extremism allowed to flourish. A government that wants to address these negative aspects of the Internet could be acting in a responsible way rather than restricting 'freedoms'.

The West, where government agencies and many firms are no angels when it comes to data collection and espionage, is seeing the rise of xenophobia, providing incontrovertible and growing evidence of governments becoming increasingly intrusive and meddling

---

[12] *The Economist*, China's social-credit system, December 17, 2016, pp. 20–22.

[13] *Financial Times*, Xi Jinping's challenge is to be strong enough to loosen control, March 25, 2015.

[14] *The Economist*, The Meddler — How Russia menaces Western democracies, February 24, 2018, p. 7.

in the daily lives of citizens. There have been highly sensitive cases, such as those highlighted by WikiLeaks and Edward Snowden, of government agencies secretly monitoring conversations and collecting private data, including on Internet use. Other examples include the CIA monitoring the private line of German chancellor Angela Merkel or the telephone bugging of Indonesian President Susilo Bambang Yudhoyono and his wife Ani by Australian authorities. What happens under the guise of national security or when government agencies clamp down on tax and social security abuse has some parallels to practices China has been criticised for.

Whilst any government intrusion into private lives is unwelcome, public anxiety in the West is coupled with a growing crisis of confidence in the current state of democracy. Many in the West are unhappy with their political system. The world's self-proclaimed leading democracy voted Donald Trump as President (with less than 25% of eligible voters endorsing him), and a small majority of Britons (but not Scots) voted for the chaos that followed Brexit in 2016. In so many ways, US presidential elections have become like farcical popularity contests influenced by the power of fundraising (a newly elected US president needs to raise hundreds of millions to finance the campaign) and the influence of powerful, well-organised special interest groups (including well-organised elites and lobbyists), which can border on something that feels like corruption. Definitions of 'corruption' can go beyond strict legal definitions, as is evident by the poor ethical behaviour and dishonest practices apparent, for example, during the GFC. Critics would argue that vested interests, be they big business or trade unions, through their financial contributions to political parties, create a contingent obligation for the account of the taxpayer. The election of President Trump highlighted how far democracy has declined, with the winning campaign resorting to unremitting lying without any electoral penalty, as evidenced by his claims that then-President Obama was not born in the US. Parallels can also be found in the scaremongering in the lead up to the Brexit vote and the tactics used in the 2016 Australian general election, when ill-founded claims were made on the privatisation of the state-sponsored health insurance scheme

Medicare. The rise of manipulative social media campaigning, electoral profiling and the collapse of any honesty or integrity from the political system, is the sobering reality that Plato feared; the collapse of democracy into ochlocracy — that self-interest and the uninformed, often populist views of many would take power. Changing these corrupting features in the US will be difficult, since the decisions by the Supreme Court in *Buckley vs. Valeo* and *Citizens United vs. FEC* argued that political donations and spending on lobbying are a form of free speech and therefore constitutionally protected (see Fukuyama, 2016).

China's critics also point to the elitism within the CCP and a sense that it is largely the domain of the privileged 'red princelings', as described by Professor Kerry Brown (2014). Such critics should reflect, however, on the influence of a small number of private schools and Oxbridge in the British establishment, the fact that France's political and industrial leadership is dominated by graduates of the three *grandes ecoles*, and that, had Hillary Clinton become the US President (she did win the popular vote by close to 3 million), the Bush and Clinton families would have provided four of the last five presidents, including second-rate presidents like George W. Bush, in the world's self-proclaimed leading democracy — a truly remarkable and statistically improbable outcome that appears almost to be caused by hereditary. These comparisons are not to defend the CCP but to provide important context.

Societal reaction to elitism in the West has been, of course, a major factor in the rise of populism. There are two separate elites: the economic elite and the cultural elite of opinion-formers. Both are often detached from broader society, particularly those who feel threatened by globalisation, immigration, and technology. Anyone sitting through a Western election campaign cannot but feel the influence of these elites as politicians are bribing their way into office with claims on taxpayers' money and promises to increase expenditures. *The Economist*[15] wrote that trust in politicians and in democracy is at an all-time low across the Western world, with a quar-

---

[15] *The Economist*, America's best hope, November 5, 2016.

ter of Americans born since 1980 believing that democracy is a bad form of government. In Australia, a 2014 Lowy Institute poll found that less than half of those aged 18–29 agreed with the statement 'Democracy is preferable to any other form of government'. A 2016 study by the Australian National University[16] revealed that Australian voters' faith in democracy had plunged to its lowest point since first being measured in 1969, with a 'popular disapproval or reaction against career politicians and everything they stand for', according to lead researcher Professor Ian McAllister. The democratic process in Australia also reveals a propensity to ditch its elected PM whenever opinion polls are heading in the wrong direction, having had 23 changes of PM without a democratic process since 1901 and five in the 10 years leading up to 2015, with three of the last four PMs deposed. In the 2015 UK election, close to 75% of eligible voters voted for a party other than the elected government.

Thucydides' Trap

At a time of social identity crisis in the West, the sense of a rising China as a threat to the US hegemony reinforces the unease and prejudice in the West and a sense of a 'Thucydides Trap', a term popularised by Professor Graham Allison (2017) to highlight the likelihood of a conflict between a rising power and an incumbent one. The term 'Thucydides Trap' has its origins in Ancient Greece. Thucydides famously said, 'It was the rise of Athens and the fear that this inspired in Sparta that make war inevitable'. The term has been used by President Xi, who said 'We all need to work together to avoid the Thucydides trap — destructive tensions between an emerging power and established powers'. That China aims to become a major power is now widely accepted. Indeed, prominent Chinese scholar Ye Zicheng captured this when he wrote, 'If China does not become a world power, the rejuvenation of the Chinese nation will be incomplete. Only when it becomes a world power can we say that the total rejuvenation of the Chinese nation has been

---

[16] www.australianelectionstudy.org.

achieved'.[17] Professor Allison suggested that, based on the history of Thucydides's Trap since the 15th century, only four of 16 cases avoided war, arguing that a war between China and the US is 'more likely than not' (Allison, 2017). Professor Shirk (2007) notes that the most notable exception to war theory occurred when the US surpassed Britain in the late 19th century. Shirk argues that war was avoided because of shared values and cultures.

In international relations theory, China is often seen as a power in transition that should be treated as a threat to American exceptionalism. Critics point to China's lack of engagement with international institutions ('free-riding' according to President Obama) but ignore the lack of involvement China had in shaping those institutions, thus seeing China as a revisionist. China's lack of engagement in world affairs is not unusual for a rising power. It took a world war to draw the US irrevocably onto the world stage in 1917 and again in 1941. Looking for evidence of a rising, overtly nationalistic and threatening China, commentators point to the growth in China's naval power, with some experts arguing that China will have as many warships as the US within a few years, with its growing ties to the Russian navy.[18] Events such as the dispute over territory in the South China Sea and the unwillingness of China to recognise the ruling against it by The Hague-based permanent court of arbitration (PCA) in 2016, highlight the sense of a more assertive China. The PCA dismissed China's 'indisputable historical claim' on sovereignty over vast areas within a 'nine-dash' line. However, seen through a different lens, China was simply following a practice adopted by the US when international agencies make a ruling contrary to US interests or sense of exceptionalism. The US, for example, refused to ratify the International Criminal Court (ICC) and the UN Convention on the Law of the Sea in 1982, when the Reagan administration argued that the convention could not take priority over domestic laws that declare American sovereignty over its surrounding seas. The Reagan administration was also unwilling to agree to the compulsory dispute

---

[17] *The Diplomat*, The Real Thucydides' Trap, Leon Whyte, May 6, 2015.
[18] *The Economist*, The new gunboat diplomacy, July 29, 2017, p. 8.

resolution mechanisms proposed by the convention, just as the Chinese were in 2016. The disregard for international institutions by the George W. Bush administration are well-documented but is ignored when criticism is made against China. Critics can often lose sight of the fact that many of the post-World War II rules-based international institutions that hold sway in global affairs, such as the United Nations, the World Bank, and the IMF, are established under the influence of the US at a time when China was excluded from having any say. China was excluded, for example, from the United Nations system until 1971, largely because of pressure from the US. China believes that major international institutions are an anachronism in need of reform so that they may better reflect the contemporary political–economic landscape, where emerging economies have greater say. China's misgivings about the mandates of such institutions in the modern era are not unreasonable and help explain, for example, the launch of the Chinese-led Asian Infrastructure Investment Bank in 2013 as an alternative to the World Bank and the Asian Development Bank.

As discussed earlier, any analysis of contemporary China and its approach to foreign affairs must understand the important role that history, particularly the Century of Humiliation, plays in the psyche of Chinese policymakers. Professor Pei (2006) noted that 'China's national experience and collective memory constitute a powerful force in foreign policy decision-making' and explained how the CCP is constantly reminding the people, particularly those in the education system, to 'never forget national humiliation' and that the CCP saved the nation. This emphasis on nationalism has allowed the CCP to position itself as the natural party to make China once more a great nation, thus strengthening its political legitimacy and popular appeal.

The progressive approach that China has taken to foreign affairs has caused much concern in the West. The guiding principle of foreign policy outlined by Deng Xiaoping in 1992, that China should 'keep a low profile [and] never take the lead', has been overtaken by the aspirations of a more confident and assertive modern China. This position has been magnified by the high profile that President Xi has taken internationally and the sense, particularly but not exclusively in the developing world, that China's financial (or 'chequebook') diplomacy has created a sense that the world is witnessing a rise in Chinese exceptionalism. In an economic sense, China is the largest trading partner to over 100 nations, some with a high level of economic dependency; a fact touched on in Chapter 2, with examples such as Pakistan and Nigeria. Thus, China's economic prospects and policies can have material implications for other nation states. Never in world history has a government had so much economic wealth to deploy to advance its foreign policy. The reality is that the economic well-being of many developing countries hinges on whether China continues with its hunger for their resources. The impact that China will have on other economies is of significance, and history informs us that the degree of political influence tends to increase along with the asymmetry of the economic relationship. For example, the temptation to deploy economic aid for strategic purposes has proven irresistible to others in the past. Is China different? To some, the risk of China as a revisionist power is real. The current reality is that China is following an independent foreign policy, and there is no evidence that China is an advocate of universal values, in the way the US promotes democracy. Western anxiety is heightened by the growing emphasis on nationalism and the assertive posture that China takes, including relationship-building with states regarded as rogue in the West (there is an old Arab saying: 'tell me who your friends are, and I will tell you who you are'). Evidence of this can be found in China's lending to some of the world's least creditworthy nations, such as Venezuela, Russia, Myanmar, Laos, Argentina, Pakistan, and Zimbabwe,[19] its close relationship with Iran, and support for North Korea. The potentially reckless nature of this chequebook diplomacy was highlighted by the plight of Venezuela, a South American country facing significant economic and political turmoil, where GDP per capita in 2017 is back at levels last seen in the 1950s and inflation rates exceed 1000%.[20] But that borrowed $65 billion from China.

---

[19] *Financial Times*, China: With friends like these, March 18, 2015.
[20] *The Economist*, Venezuela's Agony, July 29, 2017, p. 7.

Despite the predictive powers of the Thucydide's Trap, China has no modern history of being an aggressor seeking to promote universal values in the way that the US is and USSR was. The 'Five Principles of Peaceful Coexistence' have been a cornerstone of Chinese policy since 1954, when premier Zhou Enlai outlined this philosophy at the Bandung Conference. The Five Principles are:

1. Mutual respect for each other's territorial integrity and sovereignty;
2. Mutual non-aggression;
3. Mutual non-interference in each other's internal affairs;
4. Equality and cooperation for mutual benefit;
5. Peaceful coexistence.

Though over 60 years old, the Five Principles remain central to China's approach to heterodox international relations, particularly in Asia. All the evidence, sensibly assessed, supports the view that China's desire to raise its prominence in global affairs is without a desire to raise fears of hegemonic intentions. The only occasion in modern times when China exhibited any meaningful military intent was in 1966 when they shot missiles across towards Taiwan, as a result of the then President of Taiwan visiting the US. Taiwan arouses intense national emotions in China, which dates to Japan's colonisation of the island from 1895 to 1945 during the 'Century of Humiliation'.

OBOR

With parallels to the US-led Marshall Plan post World War II, the launch of the One Belt, One Road (OBOR) strategy in 2015 has seen major Chinese-sponsored investments in roads and rail links spanning across 65 countries in regions such as East India, Pakistan, Africa, and Central Asia, with the potential to profoundly change the relationship between China and Central Asia in terms of both economics and geopolitical machinations. The OBOR strategy, which focuses on five areas — infrastructure, trade, policy, finance, and people — is, the Chinese argue, a commercial initiative and not an aid programme. Yet, there is no doubt that many developing economics will benefit greatly from China's region building leadership — leadership not seen by any nation since the Marshall Plan in Western Europe. The 'belt' refers to the overland route linking China to Central Asia, Russia, and Europe, and the 'road' is a maritime one connecting China to Southeast Asia, India, and Africa. With close to $1 trillion of such projects announced as at the end of 2016 (funded by Chinese policy and commercial banks), the commercial logic and high-risk nature of the projects has been a noticeable feature. Rating agency Fitch Ratings commented that 'The lack of commercial imperatives behind OBOR projects means that it is highly uncertain whether future project returns will be sufficient to fully cover repayments to Chinese creditors'.[21] Laos, for example, is the recipient of a high-speed railway that is expected to cost $7 billion, which is more than half of the Southeast Asian country's GDP.

Soft Power

A significant weakness in China's growing international influence is its lack of soft power — the ability to influence without coercion or payment. A nation's soft power can, according to American academic and soft power guru Professor Joseph Nye (2004), come from three sources:

— culture;
— political values; and
— foreign policies (when they are legitimate and carry moral authority).

In China's case, of the three sources, transporting its political values is unlikely to carry much influence beyond a very limited market. In foreign policies and culture, however, China has much to

---

[21] *Financial Times*, China $1trn projects raise bank risk fears, January 27, 2017.

work with in rebuilding soft power, some of which — particularly culture — was on display in the memorable opening ceremony of the 2008 Olympic Games in Beijing.

Soft power is, however, not new to China. China once radiated soft power as the Middle Kingdom, where, under the tributary system, surrounding states would kowtow to the emperor and deliver tributes as a token of their esteem for the influence China exerted in Asia. In the modern era, the absence of soft power 'muscle' causes China to continue its emphasis on financial diplomacy, its chequebook foreign policy. However, promoting Chinese culture through Confucian Institutes, promoting the study of Mandarin, China's growing presence in international business and in sports, particularly football, will be just a few of the ways China will use to grow its soft power (or *ruan shili*). Estimates suggest that China is spending more than $10 billion a year on state-sponsored 'brand China' building.[22] To help promote China, the government's main news agency, Xinhua, has been expanding its international footprint, seeking to build a reputation and capabilities comparable to the BBC and CNN. In the printed media, the *China Daily* pays for inserts in publications such as the *Wall Street Journal*, *Washington Post*, and several Australian newspapers.

Tyrannies of Democracy

In his excellent book *The China Model: Political Meritocracy and the Limits of Democracy*, Daniel Bell (2015) highlighted the tyrannies of democracies, three of which I touch on here to highlight some of the flaws and problems plaguing leading Western democracies and why a crisis of confidence has taken hold. These flaws, not all equal weight, will need little elaboration for the politically aware reader.

The tyranny of the majority: Self-interested and all-powerful majorities act without regard for minority views and can enact bad policy, particularly if it is based on populism and includes a strong charismatic leader. Such a government majority can be achieved under most democratic systems without winning the popular vote.

---

[22] *The Economist*, Soft power — Buying love, March 25, 2017, p. 26.

The tyranny of the minority: Small well-organised self-interested groups are allowed to exert a disproportionate influence on the political process, including the ability to promote special-interest agendas and block important reforms to benefit their own narrow self-interest, often at the expense of broader public interests. Such power can be vested in minority parties, even when their popular vote barely registers. Recent Western elections have highlighted several examples of this at work, together with near misses.

The tyranny of the voting community: This is evident in demographic biases in voting. Thus, older voters might vote for policies that could be damaging in the future and at the cost of younger voters and those not yet eligible to vote. Arguably, Brexit is an example of this. In Singapore, there are powers vested in the President to veto laws that harm the interests of future generations (Bell, 2015: 17).

To three of Bell's tyrannies, I would add a fourth.

The tyranny of economic elites: Powerful, well-organised, and well-funded groups can promote special-interest agendas and often seek to bend the system to suit their needs. Thus, important reforms can be blocked, misleading information and media campaigns can be bought, and 'friendly' regulations and laws can be allowed to remain or be introduced, even when there is strong societal demand for change. The GFC highlighted how these elites can be resilient to the demands for change from the public and avoid any accountability for the catastrophic damage they inflict. The reputation of the banking system is unlikely to ever recover from its conduct both pre- and post-GFC.

Individually and collectively, these flaws are major factors in the crisis that faces democracy today and a major, but not the only, reason why populism is on the rise. The crisis in democracy is also fuelled by confusion between democracy, which is largely framed on national needs, and capitalism, which arguably cares little about national interest, and is essentially global in outlook. Democracy is based on the core principle of equality — one person, one vote — whereas the fruits of capitalism tend to be concentrated in the economic elite. The GFC highlighted how unbridled capitalism can create havoc on national economies and, consequently, attitudes towards to the fairness of democracies.

Selection of Political Talent Based on Meritocracy

One of the stark contrasts between liberal democracies and the 'China Model' is the rigorous process through which political leaders in China emerge. Whilst there is no doubt that networks and favouritism play a role, there is clear evidence of a political meritocracy that does not exist in the West. The central idea behind political meritocracy is that the system develops leaders of the highest quality. Bell (2015) notes:

> In theory, perhaps, the method of selecting political leaders in meritocracies via examinations and decades-long performance evaluation at lower levels of government has advantages compared to democratic systems that elect leaders in regular competitive election.

The promotion of President Xi illustrates how this system of political meritocracy works. President Xi worked his way through political offices at the township level, county level, department levels, and province-ministry level, and then entered the Central Committee, the Politburo, and then into a leadership position in the Standing Committee of the Politburo, under rigorous evaluation at each stage. Such an extensive apprenticeship allowed President Xi to not only understand the grassroots across many parts of China but also demonstrate his leadership and collaboration skills at all levels. Before attaining the highest office in the land, he was tried and tested as a proven performer. Like all ambitious officials, President Xi had to take a highly competitive set of examinations (including written and oral tests emphasising technical competence) before being considered for promotion. This system contrasts in the extreme to how, for example, President Trump became the leader of the US.

In Contrast

Whilst critics point to the lack of democracy in China, supporters of liberal values should be acutely aware of the growing societal dismay and a sense that Western democracy in its current form has run its course and is no longer fit for its purpose. Few would argue that democracy is not in a crisis. Yet given its ideological underpinning and conviction, it is a puzzle that after centuries of development, institutions of liberal democracy are in such a state of crisis. It is worth reflecting on the lack of progress made within many Western economies on nation-building investment. China produces a five-year plan, whilst some Western democracies struggle to pass an annual budget. India's failure to make economic progress highlights the contrasting nature of democratic models in complex developing economies versus the sustainable nature of 'socialism with Chinese characteristics'. The Western democratic process has created a bloated government conglomerate that has been increasingly encroaching on personal freedoms. The adage of 'beware of what you ask for, as you may get it' is a reminder of the weaknesses in democracy as foretold by Plato in *The Republic*. Plato feared that the masses were moved by emotion rather than reason and by self-serving short-term thinking rather than long-term investment. Micklethwait and Wooldridge (2014: 265) summarise the current health of democracy in the West:

> The danger to democracy's health today, at least in the West, comes in three subtle forms. The first is that the state will keep on expanding, gradually reducing liberty. The second is that the state will surrender ever more power to special interest groups. The third danger is that the state will keep making promises it cannot fulfil — creating entitlements it cannot pay for.

Deng Xiaoping, a great economic reformer and an admirer of Western economies, worried that Western political principles would produce only havoc and chaos in China (Kissinger; 2011: 444). Deng Xiaoping pointed to the US and said, 'There are three governments in the United States. When we deal with them, we do not know who can make decisions. They balance each other out and wrangle with each other. It is very difficult to get anything done' (Zhau, 2009: 252). Deng remained unwavering in his ideological commitment to the *Four Cardinal Principles*; these principles could equally be applied to the leadership philosophy of President Xi. Some in the West would affirm that Deng's concern on Western political principles, is a reality in many leading democracies, from the cradle of democracy in Greece to the world's largest economy, the US. The Chinese political system is undoubtedly flawed and in need of change, particularly regarding civil liberties and government transparency. However, do Western democratic systems of government truly present China with an alternative model? Aden and Bartels (2016) in their excellent analysis, highlight all the inadequacies of elected governments in the modern era, with the rise of populism now a serious threat to a system once seen as the holy grail of civil societies.

Checks and Balances

The counterargument is that, at a fundamental level, there is a difference between political leaders and institutions. Both democracies and authoritarian states can have poor leaders who can inflict much damage on the economy and society. In democracies, there are institutional mechanisms for dealing with bad leaders through the electoral process. In a democracy, the rule of law can act as a check and balance on a bad leader, as can the freedom of the press. The same cannot be said of China. The great British PM Winston Churchill once said, 'Democracy is the worst form of government except for all those others that have been tried'. Reflecting on Churchill's observation today, some might argue that the China model of socialism with Chinese characteristics is the 'least bad model', given how that model has performed, compared to, for example, India and most other developing nations.

At best, the evidence suggests that parliamentary democracies can work well in developed nations but that, absent some important conditions — including mature institutions — developing nations will experience problems functioning under such a system. Military coups are often features of such nations, as governments have problems exercising control. Liberal democracy for the sake of liberal democracy as defined by the West is not a formula with universal application. History, culture, and the unique characteristics of a nation should be important factors in identifying the most appropriate, or least bad, form of government; political relativism rather than absolutism. Henry Kissinger (2011) understood this when he wrote, 'China is singular. No other country can claim so long a continuous civilization, or such an intimate link to its ancient past and classic principle of strategy and statesmanship'.

The CCP is not oblivious to the issues it and China faces. During the Third Plenum in 2013, President Xi gave a candid assessment of the challenges:

> China's development faces a series of outstanding contradictions and challenges. There are still many more difficulties and problems waiting for us in the future. For example, the lack of balance, coordination, and sustainability in development is still outstanding. The capability of scientific and technological innovation is not strong. The industrial structure is not reasonable and the development mode is still extensive. The development gap between urban and rural areas and between regions is still large, and so are income disparities. Social problems have increased markedly. There are many problems affecting people's immediate interests in education, employment, social security, healthcare, housing, the ecological environment, food and drug safety, workplace safety, public security, law enforcement, and administration of justice. Some people still lead hard lives. The problems of going through formalities, bureaucratism, hedonism, and extravagant practices are outstanding. Some sectors are prone to corruption and other misconduct, and the fight against corruption remains a serious challenge for us. The key to solving these problems lies in deepening reform.

Dealing with these issues is very complex, and this complexity is evident in the defining role that culture plays, particularly in managing global markets.

5

The Complexity of Culture

Convergence of management will never come. What we can bring about is an understanding of how culture affects our thinking differently from other people's thinking and what this means for the transfer of management practices and theories.

Hofstede

In this chapter and the one on strategy that immediately follows, the important links between culture and strategy are discussed. These links are more than theoretical; they are very practical and provide a core foundation for understanding the challenges Chinese firms face in going global. Management guru Peter Drucker is purported to have said that 'culture eats strategy for lunch'. One way to interpret Drucker's quip is that, whilst strategy can and does change, culture tends to be deeply rooted and enduring; employees relate to national and firm cultures more than they might to a strategy. Culture is relevant to firms in international markets, as they tend to exhibit the dominant culture of their home market. Thus, an understanding of both strategy and cross-cultural management in an international market must be viewed as interconnected and central to success. A core reality is that cultural differences matter enormously and understanding how those differences can manifest is at the heart of good management. The cultural context in which business is done can be defining.

Culture is a complex concept that is often underestimated. Generalisations, like averages, are dangerous for understanding complex situations, just as it is dangerous for a non-swimmer crossing a river, after being told that it is only one metre deep on average, to find out that it is two metres deep in the centre; so it is with generalisations on culture. Whilst culture is not static, as it does evolve, the deep values of a culture change very slowly. The term 'culture' is used loosely in business discourse; it has many different meanings to people. Is it 'collective mental programming', 'software of the mind', 'shared assumptions', or 'shared beliefs and values'? Hofstede (1984) defined culture as 'the collective programming of the mind which distinguished the members of one human group from another'. In its simplest form, culture is how people behave in a certain situation, but culture can hide more than it reveals. On the surface, cultural differences can be apparent in dress, communication approaches, and customs, but, below the surface, it can be more difficult to understand values, beliefs, traditions, philosophies, assumptions, and communication. When comparing Anglo-Saxon and Chinese cultures superficially, the natural reaction is to be convinced that they are incompatible. From a Western perspective, Chinese language and culture can be as impenetrable as the Great Wall of China.

In understanding Chinese culture, Martin Jacques' (2009) critique highlights three important building blocks. First, China's self-identity comes from a strong history stretching back to a 'civilisation state' rather than a 'nation state'. The most important value is unity, the maintenance of the civilisation, as is evident, for example, in the categorisation of Hong Kong as 'one country, two systems' and the policy that Taiwan is and has always been an integral part of Greater China. Second, China's concept of race is linked to the civilisation state, whereby, though there are 56 ethnic groups in China, Han Chinese (who represent 92% of the population) creates an extraordinary homogeneity with a Han-centred worldview, with a very strong sense of identity. Third, the Chinese have always seen the state as playing a special role as the guardian of civilisation and patron of the family. In this context, the state in China has greater legitimacy than its equivalent in any Western nation. Both race and ethnicity are central to

China's national identity; at the same time, there are significant regional cultural and dialectal differences among north, east, south and west China. Race was a central theme at the outset of Republican China. Sun Yat-sen, widely seen as the defining leader of the modern Chinese nation promoted the idea of a 'common blood'. In a 2014 speech, President Xi emphasised this when he said, 'Generations of overseas Chinese never forget their home country, their origins or the Chinese nation flowing through in their veins'.[1] The same article highlighted the pressure placed on Chinese immigrants in Australia to support the 'motherland' and adopt the 'correct attitude' in discussions on the disputed islands in the South China Sea.

Many non-Chinese firms, business leaders, politicians and policymakers fail to appreciate the uniqueness of China and its culture. The essence of the challenges facing Western firms was encapsulated by former Australian ambassador to China Stephen Fitzgerald (2015) who wrote:

> China isn't a habit of mind for Australians. The influence it wielded it wielded in its own universe for two thousand years before the Europeans arrived is unknown. The traditional culture and the political and social concepts that influence the China we deal with are uncomprehend. The historic spread of Chinese influence is a process we do not understand. There's intrinsic worth in understanding Chinese culture for its own value ... there is a national interest in the promotion of cultural, including scholarly and research, exchange. Without this, our relations with China will never be more than superficial, and we'll be damagingly ill equipped to adjust to a China dominant in our region.[2]

The sentiment that former Ambassador Fitzgerald expressed was echoed by former Australian PM Paul Keating in 2016[3] when he

---

[1] *The Economist,* Who is Chinese? November 19, 2016, pp. 20–22.
[2] Fitzgerald's quote relates to a communication he sent in the 1970s; his prologue, however, would largely be just as relevant today.
[3] *The Australian,* Australia must heed the shift in the US–China power balance: Keating, December 24–25, 2016.

argued that Australian leaders and their advisers have failed to appreciate the transformation that has taken place because of the rise of China and are locked in an outdated world paradigm. These views, when set in a geopolitical context, are equally true in business and other settings. For example, during the visit of the Australian PM and a business delegation to China in 2016, the delegation chose to promote AFL, an indigenous sport little known outside Australia, even though President Xi has a well-known passion for football (soccer) and Australians were then the Asian Champions. When President Xi visited the UK in 2015, his passion for football was well understood by his guests, and he and the British PM visited a leading football club. In 2016, the Chinese digital broadcaster PPTV signed a record $700 million three-year television rights deal with the English Premier League. Football has the potential to do for diplomacy and international relations what table tennis did in the early 1970s to help with the thaw in Sino-US relations, that ultimately paved the way for President Nixon's historic visit to Beijing to meet Chairman Mao. The role played by the US and Chinese table tennis teams became known as 'ping-pong diplomacy'.

The Chinese have set themselves ambitious goals for football — opening 20,000 football-specific academies, investing billions of dollars in the game, and setting a goal of winning the World Cup one day, or at least becoming a football powerhouse by 2030 — thus recognising the powerful soft-power potential of a game followed by billions of people all over the world. The fact that Australians are the Asian Champions presented the Australian delegation a wonderful opportunity to promote Australia's credentials and establish cultural bonds and goodwill. The Germans, in contrast, signed a football 'treaty' as the basis of a cultural partnership. The *Financial Times* noted[4] that 'The Sino-German pact could signal a thawing of diplomatic relations, following a series of recent spats'. These simple miscalculations are symptomatic of a failure, as Fitzgerald described, 'China isn't a habit of mind for Australians'.

---

[4] *Financial Times*, China and Germany in football pact, December 2, 2016.

Whilst strategy, economics, finance, marketing, operational management, and other business disciplines are universal, culture is idiosyncratic to a nation. A deeper understanding of the role of culture is central to being able to 'stand in someone else's shoes' and foster economic development. Understanding cultural differences is not enough; managers must also know what those differences mean. The maxim of 'seek first to understand, before seeking to be understood' is sound advice, emphasising what experts call 'cross-cultural literacy'. Managers learn their culture at an early age; it represents the cumulative learning of generations. Thus, the learning is deeply rooted in the individual's unconscious values. Under pressure, managers can be predicted to default to deeply held beliefs and values. Whilst firms may have their own culture, it is influenced by the national context and, for foreign-located subsidiaries, by the Head Office (HO) context. Whether the firm culture as defined by the Chinese HO culture can supplant the culture of the nation where a newly acquired foreign subsidiary operates is critical to understanding the success of foreign investment. This is something I explore in two short case studies later in this chapter.

Research Finding

Cultural as a *soft* barrier for Western executives was revealed in the research on 54 Chinese firms operating in Australia: 84% of Chinese executives believe either very strongly or strongly, or agree, that senior management in Chinese overseas operations must understand the Chinese market, and 88% believe very strongly or strongly, or agree, that non-Chinese senior management must understand Chinese culture (Table 1).

An important insight from these findings relates to the international perspective or worldview of Chinese managers and their ability to embrace diversity, which can be viewed as a necessary condition for success in international markets. The data would suggest that the *soft* barriers to inclusion remain high, but the *hard* barriers do not (Chinese spoken language skills are used as a proxy). A hard barrier however exists within SOEs: one experienced Chinese CEO

Table 1: **Importance of Understanding Chinese Culture**

Question	Very strongly agree (%)	Strongly agree (%)	Agree (%)	Neutral (%)	Disagree (%)	Strongly disagree (%)	Very strongly disagree (%)
Senior management outside China must understand the Chinese market	31	33	20	7	6		2
Senior management in foreign subs. should have experience in working in China at HO	17	31	22	26	2	2	
Non-Chinese senior management should understand Chinese culture	28	31	30	10	2		
Non-Chinese senior management should speak Mandarin	7	11	17	43	17	2	4

Source: Healy (2015). MA Dissertation Research. See Appendix 2.

commented that the existence of barriers reflects a 'culture that distrusts outsiders'. There is much evidence that SOEs are reluctant to hire senior executives from the international market, reinforcing a suspicion that Chinese firms are insular, lack cultural diversity, and are difficult to understand.

In understanding culture, the approach of Hofstede (1996) is helpful. He argues that there is a three-layered model of culture: the first layer covers people's norms of behaviour; the second layer highlights the values that underpin those norms; and the third layer identifies the deeply held belief and assumptions that underpin those values. Critical to understanding culture and management practices in different countries is communication. Hall (1976) introduced a powerful framework for understanding culture in the form of communication through the concept of *high-* and *low-*context cultures. In *high-*context cultures (e.g. most Asian countries), relationship networks are generally long standing, and, because of a 'shared code', communication is efficient and less reliant on the detail of the written contract. In *low*-context cultures (e.g. Anglo-Saxon countries), greater emphasis is placed on the detail of the communication and the formality of the written contract. This distinction is often the cause of much misunderstanding — a common cause of failure in international markets, particularly M&A-based market entry. The important insight here is that experience and background can be a filter for effective communication: instead of hearing what is said, we hear what our mind tells us has been said, and the two can be different. The danger of cognitive dissonance, whereby you receive and accept information that is consistent with what is already a belief and reject or have difficulty with information that is inconsistent with established beliefs, is a real challenge in cross-cultural management. In dealing with China, business leaders and politicians are well advised to reflect on the advice from Cohen (2001), when he reminds us that language 'is not a neutral, transparent window through which the world reveals itself and translation cannot be a facsimile of the original'.

Hofstede's Cultural Dimensions

A helpful, though imperfect, framework for contrasting different cultures is that developed by Hofstede (1996). This framework should be understood by managers in Chinese and non-Chinese firms as it highlights important differences in key cultural dimensions: the power distance of the managers (in China, distance between people in a hierarchy is important, and inequality amongst people is expected and desired; respect and saving face are important); masculinity versus femininity (division of roles and values in society); individualism versus collectivism (highlighting, for example, the importance of guanxi in a collectivist society); the level of uncertainty avoidance (desire to avoid uncertainty, in contrast to comfort with it); and the long-term or short-term orientation of the negotiators. Using Hofstede's simple model as an indicative guide, Figure 1 illustrates the important points of cultural difference between Australia and China. Understanding these differences can be critical in ensuring cultural empathy.

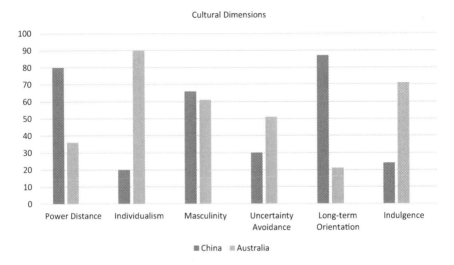

Figure 1:   Hofstede's Cultural Dimensions — China and Australia

Source: Hofstede's Cultural Dimensions (https://geert-hofstede.com).

The first measure is *power distance*, which provides a guide to the level of inequality a society accepts as a norm. A high-power distance score indicates that a society accepts an unequal, hierarchical distribution of power, whereby more powerful people are respected and often unchallenged by those less powerful. A low score means the opposite — that power is widely dispersed, and authority can be and is challenged. Consistent with Confucian values, the Chinese have greater respect for seniority and hierarchy, and the comparison with Australia (and other Anglo-American cultures) on this measure speaks for itself. In a business context, whilst Australians like Americans, consider themselves egalitarian, the Chinese, like most Asian cultures, have a respect for hierarchy and a deference to authority, which is deeply woven into the national psyche. The second measure is *individualism*, which contrasts cultures that value individualism with those that value collectivism. In the latter, people are loyal to a group, seek harmony, and wish to function as a collective. In individualist societies, greater emphasis is placed on individual achievements and recognition. Again, the contrast between China and Australia needs no commentary. The third measure is *masculinity* vs. *femininity*. Here, both the Chinese and Australasian measures are broadly in line. This measure looks to the distribution of roles between men and women and the extent to which cultural values are driven by traits normally associated with men, such as strong ego, money, and achievements, compared to more feminine values such as quality of life, relationships, and achieving consensus. The fourth measure, *uncertainty avoidance*, assesses how people cope with uncertainty and anxiety. Where the score is low, this indicates that people are more open and inclusive, with less of a sense of urgency. A high score indicates a more conservative society but also a high-energy society, where people are striving for more. The fifth measure looks at the degree to which a society values taking a *long-term relationship* and investment perspective. The contrast here is significant and demonstrates the tendency in Australia — and most Anglo-Saxon societies — for short-term results and constant measures of success versus the more measured long-term perspective taken in China. The sixth and final measure looks at the degree to which a society is *indulgent* or *restrained*. A highly indulgent society is optimistic and materialistic, and freedom of expression is the norm. In a low-indulgent or restraint society, people are more cautious, more controlled, and rigid in their behaviour. Again, the contrast between Australia and China speaks for itself. In aggregate, this simple framework for comparing different cultures can be revealing regarding the degree to which differences may exist and the level of skill and empathy that need to be adopted to avoid misunderstanding and, ultimately, failure.

For Australian (and other Anglo-American) managers, politicians, and policymakers, in order to be well prepared in their relationship building and negotiation with their Chinese counterparts, an appreciation of the differences highlighted by Hofstede's framework is essential.

Complimentary to Hofstede's framework, another important contextual area of difference was described by Scarborough (1998), who compares Chinese and Western cultures and finds that the latter has an 'aggressive, active approach to nature, technology and progress, with a reliance on logical and scientific methods' — many of the traits traditionally associated with Western MBA training. The Chinese culture, in contrast, is found to be 'passive, fatalistic, with a reliance on precedent, intuition and wisdom', influenced greatly by Confucian values. The lasting influence of Confucian values has endured in China despite efforts under the leaders of the iconoclastic May Fourth Movement, or the 'new culture' movement (*Mr Democracy, Mr Science*), which began around 1916 as an anti-imperialist, cultural, and political student movement but then sparked into life through student protests in Beijing on May 4, 1919.[5] The May Fourth Movement led to the early momentum to eradicate traditional culture, which then became an important theme under Mao Zedong, who viewed traditional culture as an obstruction to the socio-economic progress China needed to become a modern nation. The rallying slogan of the CCP then was to 'Smash Confucianism' (*zalan Kongjia dian*). From 1949 and through the Cultural Revolution, Mao Zedong set about overthrowing the value system of an entire society, which he saw as feudal, as he sought to eradicate the 'Four Old's' — *old ideas, old culture, old customs,* and *old habits.* However, changing a culture is not easy: during the Cultural Revolution, Mao Zedong candidly acknowledged that it was hard for people to overcome the habits of 3,000 years (Edgar, 1971).

The deep-seated nature of culture in China can be understood by the fact that China has one of the longest-lasting civilisations and one that is furthest from Westphalian ideas. Operating a tribute system for many centuries, the Chinese long held the view that China, or more precisely the Emperor, ruled over 'All Under Heaven' and that China in a hierarchical sense defined the highest order of civilisation. In terms of historical context, Chinese people have historically, and for good reason, been wary of foreigners. As described earlier, the Century of Humiliation is deeply ingrained in the psyche of Chinese people given the long and violent history

---

[5] The May Fourth Movement is the name given to the demonstrations provoked by the Treaty of Versailles, which was viewed as unfair to China. The Movement marked the shift towards the ideals of the Russian Revolution and away from traditional ideals. The CCP identifies the Movement as its intellectual origin.

of foreign invaders from the 1840s until the establishment of the People's Republic of China in 1949.

Unlike some Western cultures, the Chinese have never seen themselves as imposing their culture and values on others on a journey to a Chinese exceptionalism. Premier Wen Jiabao summarised this view:

> We must recognise the multiplicity of world cultures, and different cultures must not exhibit prejudice, enmity or rejection of each other but must respect each other and learn from each other working together to form a harmonious and varied civilisation. (Fewsmith, 2010)

The Influence of Confucianism

Ironically, the CCP has been at the vanguard of a revival of Confucianism, which is now fully incorporated in official discourse and plays a central role in the promotion of Chinese soft power through Confucian Institutes, which can be found throughout the world, often aligned to a university. Confucianism was officially rehabilitated following the promotion in 2005 by President Hu Jintao of the 'Harmonious Society' social movement, which was based on Confucian philosophy. The influence of Confucian values on Chinese culture cannot be underestimated, and it is now promoted, together with other Chinese traditions and cultural norms, as an important part of Chinese modernity. Confucian beliefs are based on a stable and enduring social order, which imposes principles on how people should behave, as distinct from the rigid laws and regulations often evident in the West. Confucians highlight four virtues governing human behaviour: *sincerity, benevolence, filial piety,* and *propriety.* Confucius defined five principal relationships:

— between a ruler and ruled;
— between husband and wife;
— between parents and children;
— between older and younger brothers; and
— between friend and friend.

Adherence to these hierarchies underpins social harmony. Confucius advocates a paternalistic governance framework, wherein leaders lead by example, and there are hierarchical systems within society and within business, where respect for seniors often calls for unquestioned obedience and where protocol ranks are important. Thus, in a business setting, challenges by subordinates would rarely occur, and protocol ranks dictate that senior Chinese executives must be met by executives from other firms of equivalent standing — Chairman to Chairman, CEO to CEO — highlighting the emphasis in Chinese culture on social status (*shehui dengji*). The moral and ethical values of the leader are important, as the following quote from the teachings of Confucius make clear: 'If a ruler himself is upright, all will go well without orders; but if he himself is not upright, even though he gives order they will not be obeyed'.[6] An important cultural difference between the West and China regards dealing with disputes. Unlike Anglo-Saxon societies, the Chinese are not litigious. Confucian values do not naturally seek 'formal' laws governing business transactions, as Miles (2006) notes:

> There is a preference in the West for arm's length, as opposed to relationship-based transactions. When a dispute arises, parties invoke their legal rights and are willing to resort to litigation … How does a corporate governance model embodying all these traits fit in with Confucian beliefs? The truth is that to a large extent, it does not.

The intangible practice of *guanxi* is also rooted in Confucianism, promoting cultural aspects of collectivism and the importance of personal networks and social capital to interpersonal relations. *Guanxi* has been the lifeblood of personal relationships and business conduct in Chinese society. A *guanxi* relationship network is often idiosyncratic to the firm. Park and Luo (2001) describe *guanxi* as 'delicate fibres woven into every person's social life and every aspect

---

[6] Excerpt from the Analects, compilation of the teachings of Confucius.

of Chinese society'. *Guanxi* is also seen as a way to mitigate the weaknesses in the legal system, as an executive at a chemical company in Zhejiang Province noted: 'There are so many problems with legal implementation. It is easier to get together a circle of friends who inform on each other and whoever dares to do something bad, everyone will know' (Nee and Opper, 2012). Linked to *guanxi* is the importance of saving face (*mianzi*), which in Chinese culture is very important. *Mianzi* is an intangible form of personal status that is imperative to maintain in cultivating *guanxi*. It defines a person's place in the social network, as Graham and Lam (2003) emphasise:

> In Chinese business culture, a person's reputation and social standing rest on saving face. If Westerners cause the Chinese embarrassment or loss of composure, even unintentionally, it will be disastrous. The Chinese notion of saving face is closely associated with American concepts of dignity and prestige.

An equally important philosophy in Chinese culture is *renqing*, which denotes an informal social obligation, normally in the form of reciprocity to others. When one member of a *guanxi* ignores the obligation for reciprocity, this can result in the loss of face, perceived as a lack of commitment, and may ultimately weaken the *guanxi*. This is an important concept when evaluating gifts such as political donations and what is implicit in the giving of such gifts.

These important, deep-rooted cultural norms are regularly misunderstood by Western executives and politicians and cause relationships to fail to realise their potential.

Negotiation Style

A useful way to highlight the role of culture in a business setting is in the theories of negotiation covering social exchange theory, game theory, and cross-cultural theory. Social exchange theory is based on win–win agreements; negotiations are based on agreed principles and are conducted in a relationship setting of trust, where tricks, games, and posturing are avoided. Game theory presupposes competitive tension and results in winners and losers; thus, tricky tactics, posturing, and sometimes deception are part of this approach. Trust is missing in such negotiations, and lasting relationships rarely evolve. Cross-cultural theory proposes that differences in cultural backgrounds impact negotiating behaviour.

Miles (2003) summed it up this way: 'Cross-cultural research focused on negotiation has clearly and conclusively demonstrated that assumptions and behaviours differ in fundamental ways across cultural boundaries'. Managers who believe that they can 'force' others to accept their cultural perspective in negotiations are likely to fail. Moreover, management optimism that cultures can be radically changed by management actions 'has been greatly reduced by experience of failure' according to Mead and Andrews (2009). This is an important and timeless insight: understanding Chinese culture is a non-trivial element of building relationships.

The major implication of cross-cultural theory is that it is highly relevant for Chinese firms in foreign markets. If negotiators do not understand this, the prospects of success are reduced. The root cause of failure, as argued by Graham and Lam (2003), is the inability of Westerners to understand the 'much broader context of Chinese culture and values'. The cultural roots of the Chinese negotiation style are a reflection of traditional culture and contemporary political culture. Chinese traditional culture is based on Confucianism and agrarian values, reflecting the fact that most urban Chinese were raised in the country and that, during the Cultural Revolution, many urban students were sent to the countryside to be 're-educated'. The contemporary political culture reflects the bureaucratic legacy of Mao Zedong, which resulted in a high level of centralisation and a risk-averse bureaucracy that sought to avoid mistakes. Mao Zedong's legacy was tempered by the more pragmatic and decentralised philosophy of Deng Xiaoping, but the roots of Mao Zedong's legacy remain deep and may be strengthened through authoritarian control under President Xi. All this adds to complexity, which Fang (2006) describes as 'a paradoxical personality. Mao Zedongist bureaucrat in learning, a Confucian gentleman and a Sun Tzu-like strategist'.

National Business Culture

It is important to understand when national culture can be a significant factor, as Tang and Ward (2003: 36) argue:

> Quite different constraints and opportunities face the Chinese manager from those confronting their counterparts in Western economies. Chinese managers not only come from a different world in terms of cultural heritage they bring with them to the job. They also find themselves inhabiting a different world in terms of the business system.

Chinese firms, for example, are more likely than Western firms to operate within a rigid hierarchical structure with many management layers and a culture that obeys rather than constructively challenges; few non-Chinese executives succeed in the higher ranks of Chinese firms. Given that cross-cultural management is critical to successful strategy execution, it is important to explore culture and ask whether Chinese firms run the risk of failure in their endeavour to build international businesses because of a lack of cultural appreciation. Hill (2011) argues that cultural differences are critical to understanding business in China:

> Beneath the veneer of Western modernism, long-standing cultural traditions rooted in a 2,000-year-old ideology continue to have an influence on the way business is transacted. (Hill, 2011)

Much of the literature on cross-cultural management places emphasis on the dominance of the national business system (NBS), where the dynamics of nationality has resulted in distinctive national paths to internationalisation. Whilst firm-specific culture is influenced by the dominant national culture, firms can develop a stronger culture than that generally associated with the national culture. For example, through its in-house management training college, GE built a distinctive culture that defines GE globally. The same is true of firms such as Goldman Sachs, McKinsey, IBM, JP Morgan, and McDonalds, to name just a few. In his best-selling book *Built to Last*

(1994), Jim Collins wrote that one of the things that successful companies have in common is a 'cult-like culture' and traditions that are unique to the firm. Experienced Western international firms have learnt to adapt their cultures to local market conditions, often by hiring local senior management. International firms perform better when their foreign subsidiary's culture is congruent with the national culture of the country it is based in. National Australia Bank (NAB), for example, focused its cross-border M&A on the UK, US and New Zealand in the 1990s because of its comfort in dealing in Anglo-American markets. However, a 'one-size-fits-all' firm culture that suggests that a good manager in Australia will be a good manager in other countries is flawed. Of the Chinese firms, Huawei has led by example in trying to internationalise their culture, reflected in the fact that a growing number of their employees are based overseas and are non-Chinese. It is thus not a surprise that, amongst large Chinese firms, Huawei has been growing in developed economies. Professor Nolan (2014) asks 'Is Huawei the "exception that proves the rule" or the "shape of things to come"'?

The criticality and complexity of cross-cultural management and the tendency to dismiss it as an HR issue highlights the need for it to be viewed as core management competencies and ongoing education requirement for senior international managers. Firms that allow culturally insensitive managers loose in foreign markets put at risk their prospects of success and reputation. The research in Table 1 underscores this critical condition with the importance of non-Chinese managers' understanding of Chinese culture, with 89% responding, 'very strongly agree', 'strongly agree', or 'agree'.

Two Case Studies: TCL and QJ

As experienced international managers know, it is one thing to buy established businesses in foreign markets and another to successfully integrate them and create value. The capabilities needed to do this are experience-based. Many of the issues facing Chinese firms in the international economy are brought to life by the case studies below involving two Chinese firms, TCL and QJ, both of which

TCL was founded in Huizhou, Guangdong province, in 1981 as an SOE. The firm grew into a well-known conglomerate and a leading brand in China across a range of sectors, with a market share of 21% for TV sets, a strong position in fixed-line telephones and with interests in other consumer electronics. The TCL leadership saw international expansion as critical to their future growth, with focus on owning brands. They successfully expanded internationally, largely in emerging markets through joint ventures (JVs) and licensing in Europe. TCL, through its JV with France's Thomson Group, became the world's largest manufacturer of TV sets, with a 9.2% market share. It would ultimately buy Thompson out of its stake in the JV. The firm described its core competences as deep customer insights into the Chinese TV market and its efficient global supply chain management. TCL set itself the goal of becoming a globally known brand for TVs and mobile phones: 'We are determined to become the Chinese Sony or Samsung' said the CEO in an interview with *The Economist*. The firm saw branding as part of its competitive advantage.

When, in 2002, German Schneider Electronics announced bankruptcy, TCL took the opportunity to accelerate its growth in Europe. The firm's chairman noted 'The chance to purchase a truly global colour-television firm just doesn't come along every day... developing a brand would have cost a large amount of money'. The Chinese government strongly supported the overseas acquisitions with cheap bank loans, tax incentives, and 'other special policies'. Buoyed by the Schneider acquisition, TCL set itself the goal of expanding through further acquisitions, with one of the criteria being that any firm acquired should 'have a similar corporate culture to ours at TCL'.

Four years after the Schneider, a TCL corporate communications executive said that they prefer not to talk about Schneider: 'It was a try. I cannot say it was successful'. Industry observers said that TCL's overall weak German market know-how and their replacement of local managers by Chinese managers were major reasons for failure. When they made the acquisition, TCL agreed to keep all the staff and German management. However, when the TCL CEO tried to contact the German executive on a Saturday, he could not reach him. As a consequence, the TCL CEO replaced the German executive with a Chinese executive 'who is available 24 hours'. This change of management was

(Continued)

(Continued)

viewed as a major reason for the business' failure. Another factor was the fact that Schneider was a loss-making business and, according to the *Financial Times*, TCL 'misjudged its power to turnaround a loss making business'. The TCL spokesperson acknowledged that, for a 'traditional Chinese firm like TCL, we do not have much experience in global markets'. Problems also soon emerged with TCL's 100% acquisition in its JV with French group Thomson. The Group CEO acknowledged that 'We do not deny that cultural differences exist between the two'. TCL decided that, if it was to develop an 'international culture', all management levels were required to learn English and to use English as the corporate language.

Source: The above notes are based on Bell, S. 2008, *TCL Corporation: International Brand Management of Chinese Companies*, Heidelberg: Physica-Verlag.

QJ, situated in Wenling, China, is a leading producer and seller of a broad range of motorcycles, holding 5% of the highly competitive Chinese market, where the market leader, Jiangmen Grand River, has 16.2%. Bco, a family-owned Italian manufacturer of motorcycles, had seen its domestic market subject to intense competition from Japanese manufacturers. As a consequence, its businesses started to decline in 1989. It was eventually purchased by QJ in 2005. QJ's motivation for the acquisition, according to a China-based senior executive was the following: 'the cost to us of developing a new product would be much higher than the price paid for Bco, and we aimed to get access to the European market, where Bco provided us with a promising platform'. QJ had no distinctive competitive advantage when entering the European market, and its goals were consistent with many Chinese firms expanding in foreign markets: to deploy competitive disadvantages in managerial skills and technology innovation. Both QJ and Bco were strangers to the foreignness of different national cultures and business practices. After the acquisition, QJ made significant investments in Bco to increase capacity and improve efficiency, and emphasis was placed on a localisation strategy, including autonomy over daily operations. The 45 employees

(Continued)

(Continued)

of Bco were retained, and 60 new employees were hired. Three Chinese expatriates arrived at Bco: the managing director (MD), the sales director, and a parts quality manager. No other job titles were changed, and Italian work practices and other symbols were left intact. The Chinese executives quickly adapted to the Italian work ethic, including the number of 'religious holidays' after an initial attempt to 'encourage workers to work longer hours'. The Chinese owners understood the importance of retaining key personnel, particularly the technical director, as the economics of the acquisition depended on access to technical knowledge. The Chinese MD encouraged cross-national learning and teamwork, but this was resisted by the local employees. One shop-floor worker complained about 'language and culture' problems and that 'communication with the Chinese technicians was never direct, which led to misunderstanding and mistakes'. The emphasis on teamwork was also resisted, as illustrated in comments from an Italian employee: 'Italian people are more focused on being individuals and always want to be the best…we do not have problems when we work with Italian people, but with Chinese people. They lack knowledge, and when they do their ways, it often turns out to be wrong'. Another local employee commented that 'I do not want to be negative, but sometimes we have problems. You know, the knowledge of the motorcycle is missing in Chinese people'. Other cultural difference soon emerged. The Italians thought the Chinese were too cost-oriented, and the decision to source less-expensive parts from China rather than Japan also incurred criticism: 'sometimes we receive parts from Chinese suppliers that are not workable. Chinese parts are less expensive, but they need to understand that, for extra cost, we would make much better motorcycles'. Increasing tension with HO led to greater centralised decision making. The Italian CFO saw this as an issue of 'low trust': 'They do not consult us. All decisions are now made by Chinese managers'. The Chinese executives at HO disagreed with the notion of centralised decision making: 'we acquired Bco and allow them to run semi-autonomously. We focus on the strategic issues and monitor how our investment is performing'.

Source: This case study draws heavily on Zhu and Wei.[7]

---

[7]Zhun and Wei (2014: 166–175), the authors of the QJ case, adopted a single interview-based case study of QJ and its acquired Italian subsidiary, Bco, which they argue 'represents a typical trajectory of how Chinese companies are involved in the overseas direct investment (ODI)'.

entered international markets through M&A. Although management capabilities are not explicitly featured in the case studies, greater knowledge of the issues — particularly cross-cultural management — may have led to different outcomes in both cases.

The TCL and QJ cases highlight many of the cultural challenges facing Chinese firms in integrating foreign acquisitions. The strategy of 'internationalisation through localisation' is consistent with the approach in the Bartlett and Ghoshal (2002) model and has been adopted by several Chinese firms such as Haier and Huawei. This is logical, given that the strategic intent of the investment is often to acquire expertise and knowledge. However, the failure to achieve effective integration, an integral part of good execution, is a weakness in the approach taken by many Chinese firms. This is largely due to a lack of capabilities and experience in managing international acquisitions and can determine whether an acquisition succeeds. The advice of former GE CEO Jack Welch, (2005) who led hundreds of acquisitions both domestically and internationally, reminds firms of the *six major pitfalls* of acquiring a business and the important role that culture plays, together with strong execution capabilities:

1. Believing that a merger of equals can occur
2. Focusing intently on strategic fit and failing to assess cultural fit ('which is just as important to success, if not more so');
3. Entering the 'reverse hostage situation' in which the acquirer ends up making so many concessions that the acquired ends up dictating key terms;
4. Integrating too timidly;
5. The conqueror syndrome, in which the acquiring company marches in and installs its own managers everywhere, undermining trust and confidence whilst potentially alienating key critical talent in the acquired firm;
6. Paying too much.

Weak integration is a feature of Chinese acquisitions and is consistent with Welch's observations, as is the importance of cultural difference, which can lead to tension, and the need for the HO to be more actively engaged in protecting the firm's investment, which in turn can create a sense of disempowerment within the subsidiary. The risks are that the business may lose momentum as a 'them vs. us' mindset sets in and key personnel may decide to leave, weakening the strategic rationale for the investment. *The Financial Times*[8] captured the essence of the complexity of culture and how it translates into the performance of the business:

> China's own business culture offers little by way of practice for working with western companies. Extreme reverence for corporate hierarchy in a country where bosses are also known as *zong*, or chief, can be suffocating … rigid obedience can inhibit suggestions from the on-the-ground teams, compounding weaknesses in due diligence, local knowledge and cultural understanding. All this helps explain the fact that about two-thirds of overseas deals by Chinese acquirers run into trouble.

A similar sentiment was expressed by Yip and McKern (2016):

> People in China like to follow a strong leader with passion and drive. So although Chinese executives recognize that they must give employees real decision-making power and push responsibility further down the organization, they struggle against a long history. The one-directional mode of instruction in the Chinese education system reinforces the culture of waiting for commands from the boss.

Despite the original good intent, the NBS effect prevails, confirming that Chinese firms are likely to adopt business practices that are deeply embedded in practices developed in their home market and thus follow a distinctive national path to

---

[8] *Financial Times*, Chinese investors take a tumble on the global stage, October 31, 2016.

internationalisation — a form of path dependency. Thus, the preference for clearly defined workplace roles and hierarchies often means that Chinese firms do not adapt well to cultures that prize decentralisation and individual initiative, creating the ingredients for repeated culture clashes between Chinese management and their Western subsidiary or partner.

Deep-rooted cultural issues were highlighted in the primary research, when one internationally experienced Chinese CEO commented that 'I have a feeling that Chinese businesses will never be truly global as they are trapped in their own culture and Chinese way of doing things. The 'family run' culture distrusts outsiders'. In this context, the weaknesses in two of the Four Cs — cultural adaptability and country of origin — are starkly highlighted.

These weaknesses in international expansion can be exaggerated by what can often appear to be a lack of strategic logic.

6

International Strategy

Hide our capacities and bide our time, but also get some things done (tao guang yang hui you sou zou wei).

Crossing the river by feeling for stones.

Deng Xiaoping

Closely linked to the complexity of culture is the theory and practice of successful international strategy, which is explored through the lens of the Four Cs of sustained competitive advantage in international markets — *core capabilities, cultural adaptability, competencies of management,* and *country of origin*. Using this framework, I assess how well-equipped Chinese firms are to overcome the challenges they face.

At the outset, three related questions should be considered regarding how Chinese firms can be internationally successful. The first question is 'Absent FSAs in successfully entering new markets, does Chinese management have the *human capital* (know-how, education, ability, and experience) to create economic value from their investments?' The second question is 'Beyond exporting, are the CSAs in terms of factor-endowment (e.g. people, lower manufacturing costs, money) enough?' The third, related question is 'How can Chinese management escape its own unique, arguably inward-looking, national culture while integrating into global markets?'

The strategy literature, which is overwhelmingly based on Western thinking and evidence, largely agrees on the importance of a firm having or acquiring a competitive advantage or FSAs, which allow it to compete and grow profitably domestically and then internationally. Challenging this thinking, Boisot and Meyer (2008) raised an important question on the relevance of current theories to Chinese firms: 'Do the current theories of internationalization offer us the right kind of guidance for dealing with the challenges posed by an internationalizing China? And if not, would we be better off seeking a more 'China-specific' theory to account for the Chinese case, or should we consider a comprehensive rethinking of our existing theories?' In a similar vein, Alon and McIntyre (2008) have argued that new or augmented theories may be needed to explain the Chinese case because China's unique institutional environment requires new approaches to understand the international strategy of Chinese firms.

Notwithstanding the arguments that China specific theories should be developed, and agreeing with Rugman (2010), who argues that traditional theories of why firms internationalise provide sufficient explanatory power and thus there is no need for new theories, a central argument in this book is that the fundamentals underpinning business success in competitive markets are universal. In supporting the relevance of universal theories for Chinese firms, it is important to acknowledge that the institutional environment for Chinese firms is unique. Mainstream strategy theory, drawing heavily from the resource-based theory of the firm, is well suited to evaluate Chinese firms in the global economy, informs us that, for a business to sustainably succeed, three interrelated conditions are essential: first, a clear sense of core capabilities-based comparative advantage (either FSA or CSA); second, the management capabilities, the *human capital*, needed to execute on a strategy; and third, access to the right mix of debt and equity capital to navigate business cycle volatility and finance growth. In two of these three, elements of the Four Cs stand out.

At a fundamental level, Michael Porter (1980), emphasising the importance of innovation to sustaining competitive advantage, also argued that 'the five forces' in an industry (such as competitive rivalry, entry barriers, and the bargaining power of suppliers and customers) mean that a firm must enjoy either a cost advantage or product differentiation such as well-known brands have if it is to avoid getting 'stuck in the middle'. If competition is intense or market conditions challenging, a firm can look to international markets that have more favourable conditions and some Privately-Owned Enterprises (POEs) have done this. If a firm internationalises its operations for that reason, it may find that other domestic competitors will follow, as 'herding' behaviours influence the strategies of rivals, who all suffer from the same domestic market conditions. To understand the scope of the internationalising strategy of Chinese firms, taking a resource-based view as the basis of an FSA is helpful. A resource-based view suggests that the firm possesses distinctive, specific core capabilities/competencies, including assets that are valuable and difficult to replicate, and that these resources are relevant to a market (i.e. the foreign market the firm is entering). Thus, a firm's ability to grow profitably is defined by market conditions and its own internal resources, including, and perhaps especially, the quality of management. Hamel and Prahald (1996) summed the situation up this way:

> Management will be judged on how well they identify, cultivate and exploit core competencies that will make sustainable growth possible. Core competencies are the collective learning of an organisation; cultivating core competencies is the best way to prevail in global competition.

A critical part of a firms' core competencies are its knowledge resources, including its managerial human capital and its social capital (*guanxi*), that is the network of relationships in other markets. The growth of POE investment in Southeast Asia — Indonesia, Hong Kong, Malaysia. Singapore, Taiwan, Thailand, and the Philippines, can be explained by social networks (Alon *et al.*, 2015).

The Why and The How

Much has been written on *why* Chinese firms are becoming more international, but less has been said about *how* this is happening, particularly regarding the importance of management capabilities, including experience in cross-border M&A. On the *why*, both theory and practice suggest the following:

For *market-seeking* Outbound Foreign Direct Investment (OFDI), this is normally done to access distribution networks to channel exports from China into foreign markets and, together with knowledge and strategic-asset seeking, can be viewed as a move to deploy competitive disadvantages. Thus, the size and stage of the economic development of the market are important factors in evaluating options. The single European market, with a population of some 500 million, would be more attractive than, say, Australia, with its population of 24 million. This is consistent with the research by Tuong Anh and Hung (2016), which shows that Chinese OFDI were strongly influenced by market-size variables, including GDP, GDP per capita, and openness to trade (Tuong *et al.*, 2016).

For *resource-seeking* OFDI, the primary motivation is to secure natural resources, energy, and food resources, which are in short supply in the domestic market. Thus, China's focus on Australia is in part motivated by its abundance of natural resources and agriculture. A number of Chinese firms, such as CITIC, have acquired natural resource assets. Investments in oil, mining, and gas in developing economies by Sinopec and PetroChina illustrate this motivation. The acquisition of the Darwin Port by Chinese company Landbridge is another example. Chinese investors also look to New Zealand because of its world-class dairy, meat, and wine sectors.

For *knowledge-seeking* OFDI, the motivation is to acquire capabilities, including superior technology, that exist in foreign markets, but which are lacking or in short supply in China. Thus, the acquisition of Australian construction company John Holland Constructions by China Communications Construction company (CCC), headed by Chairman Liu Quitao, a close associate of President Xi, gave the Chinese firm strong technical and project management expertise in large-scale infrastructure projects. Lenovo's acquisition of IBM's ThinkPad business was motivated by the desire to acquire expertise in laptop computing, given the huge potential in China and elsewhere. Huawei Technologies invests heavily in overseas R&D to track cutting-edge developments and introduce its management to advanced technology in developed markets (Huawei has 18 integrated R&D centres ('labs') in Stockholm, Dallas, Silicon Valley, Bangalore, Moscow, and Helsinki as well as in several locations within China). Huawei's vision of the future includes using cloud computing as a way to go from being a telecommunication equipment firm to a broader-based supplier of IT services, challenging HP Enterprises, Cisco, and IBM. Goodbaby, the world's largest producer of strollers and baby carriages, has established design and technical centres in China, Europe, the US, and Japan. When Haier bought Fisher & Paykel, it was because of the New Zealand firm's world-class production expertise.

For *strategic asset-seeking* OFDI, the motivation is (for similar reasons) to acquire capabilities such as brands that would take considerable time, investment, and risk to build domestically. This motive explains TCL's purchase of the European TV set business discussed in Chapter 5. Zhejiang Geely Group's acquisition of Volvo had a combination of brand and technical expertise as the motivation. When Fosun, a privately owned Chinese conglomerate, invested in Club Med, a major driver was to support Western brands expanding into China. Fosun could allow Club Med access to its relationship networks in China. HNA's acquisition of US technology product company Ingram Micro saw the firm surge in growth from its Chinese operations, which, despite a 20-year presence in China, struggled to make meaningful progress until the change of ownership.

Several other theories can help explain why a firm might internationalise its operations, but, except for the institutional theory, they are less relevant to most Chinese firms.

In *order-driven theory*, the customer demand for a firm's products and services can motivate a move away from a pure export model to one with an in-market presence to support export activity, provide on-the-ground customer service, and increase in-market share.

In *customer-driven theory*, the strategy of key customers causes a firm to follow their customers into key foreign markets. This is a justification for service firms like banking, management consulting, and law firms to expand in tandem with their customers, so that they protect their relationships and remain relevant to their customers.

In *competition-driven theory*, 'herding instincts' will cause firms to follow major competitors into new markets for fear of missing out. Examples include McDonald's and KFC, Coca-Cola and Pepsi-Cola, McKinsey & Co. and BCG, and Citibank and JP Morgan.

Transaction cost theory argues that firms internationalise to reduce their costs. Evidence of this theory can be found in Chinese inbound foreign direct investment (IFDI), where Western firms have taken advantage of China's comparative advantage through its abundance of low-cost labour.

In *institutional theory*, a firm may decide to escape conditions in the domestic market that constrain or add higher costs by entering more favourable markets. Conversely, there may be incentives from the government encouraging firms to internationalise their operations. Such incentives could include subsidised and generous loans, grants, tax incentives, and soft budget constraints.

Theory to Practice

As highlighted by theory, firms invest in foreign markets for a variety of reasons. In practice, the most common reasons and how they might explain the international strategy of Chinese firms can be summarised as in Table 1.

This simple analysis shows that the most likely motivation is that of gaining a foothold in an important economic block such as the European Union as well as the acquisition of technology and management know-how. Other factors include the pursuit of long-term, sustainable growth and seeking a more favourable regulatory and financing environment that appeals to POEs.[1] There are a range of other explanations — particularly for POEs, as discussed later — such

---

[1] *China's Increasing Outbound M&A*, JP Morgan Insights, 2016.

Table 1: Some Common Reasons for OFDI

Strategic rationale	Explanation for Chinese firms
Increase sales and profits	Unlikely
Benefit from rapid growth outside home market	Unlikely
Reduce costs	Unlikely
Gain foothold in economic blocks (e.g. Europe)	Highly likely
Protect domestic markets	Unlikely
Protect foreign markets	Unlikely
Acquire technology and management know-how	Highly likely
Avoid adverse conditions at home	Likely
Diversification of economic and political risk	Likely

Table 2: Motivations for Chinese Firms' Foreign Investment

Motivation	Number of articles	% of total
Acquisition of foreign strategic assets	17	74
Response to government actions	13	57
Exploitation of foreign strategic assets	11	48
Access to raw materials	9	39
Search for new markets	9	39
Institutional escapism	7	30
Diversification	5	22
Total	**23[a]**	

Note: [a]For Tables 2, 4, and 5, the number of articles do not add up to 23 (or 100%) because some studies analyse more than one motive for international expansion.
Source: Rosch (2013, p. 55).

as those highlighted by several studies on the motivations of Chinese firms entering foreign markets. Rosch (2013), for example, conducted a review of research articles on the motivation and management of entry mode together with the challenges of the liability of foreignness for Chinese firms in foreign markets (Table 2).

Rosch's research, which was largely SOE-based, provides strong evidence supporting the acquisition and exploitation of foreign strategic assets (74% and 48%, respectively). Consistent with the Fifth C hypothesis, an important insight is the influence of government (57%), which is consistent with the *go global* directive in 1999 and the 2012 directive from President Hu Jintao that *Chinese companies should expand their overseas presence at a faster rate.* Related to this is the concept of 'institutional escapism', which features strongly at 30%. Implicit in the term 'institutional escapism' is the notion of constraints being placed on the firm by institutional arrangements in its domestic market. These constraints can be formal or informal, reflecting societal values as well as laws, rules, and regulations at national or local levels. Institutional escapism can also provide a rationale where corruption is a cost or where there is weak protection of intellectual property rights.

Much of the Chinese OFDI has historically been *resource-seeking* and *market-seeking.* This strategic logic helps explains several puzzles, such as why Chinese firms need to compete abroad given that the domestic market is so vast. It is easier to grow economies of scale at home, with a population of 1.35 billion with a growing middle class. Regardless of motivation, as any firm expanding into new geographies will attest, an international strategy is more complex than a domestic strategy. These complexities are even greater for Chinese firms seeking cultural integration, as foreign markets lack social or strategic networks. The role and power of informal networks in China act as substitutes for formal legal structures and institutions. As Gulati *et al.* (2000) note, 'the networks of relationships in which firms are embedded profoundly influence their conduct and performance'. This insight is particularly important for China, where *guanxi* underpins networks and where relational capital reduces transaction costs, establishes legitimacy, and compensates for institutional weaknesses, whilst providing access to resources that might otherwise be difficult to obtain. Establishing network linkages in foreign markets is not easy and requires much commitment of resources and cultural dexterity, adding greatly to the transaction costs of internationalising a firm.

These complexities also exist where the primary motivation for the internationalisation strategy is to develop capabilities to be employed in China in order to create or strengthen a domestic competitive advantage. There is sound logic to the argument that a key motivation for some Chinese firms is to acquire expertise and assets in foreign markets that can then be readily employed domestically. The economic evaluation of foreign investment must also be viewed through that lens, though how this is ultimately assessed will depend greatly on management capabilities in integrating the acquisition and in transferring knowledge. A positive paradigm would see this as a natural next stage in the opening up of Chinese markets and the desire to create an innovation-focused business landscape. Free-market economists have long argued that the globalisation of trade and competition creates the opportunity for domestic firms to learn from developed-economy firms in areas such as management, project management, technical know-how, human resource management, corporate financing, marketing, and brand management.

Do POEs Have Different Motivations?

A study by Wen and Liyun (2015) on the motivation for internationalising business operations of 16 POEs revealed insights consistent with hypothesis that (at least for POEs) entrepreneurship into foreign markets can be viewed as a form of *crossing the river by feeling for stones* (Table 3).

The survey shows that at least 10 of the 16 firms regarded entrepreneurship as the most important motivation for expanding into foreign markets, with no other factor coming a close second (a broader definition of 'entrepreneurship' would suggest that 12 out of the 16 firms had this motivation). In an unpublished PhD thesis, Cen (2013) highlights that Chinese entrepreneurs investing in Australia do so from a 'welfare-seeking motivation'. This motivation is to enjoy the better quality of life offered in Australia, including a world-class education system, health care, relatively environmentally unpolluted first-world living standards, and an environment less competitive than that in China. The Australian government requires Chinese entrepreneurs to invest a minimum of A\$5 million in a new business in order to obtain the necessary resident visas, a hurdle

Table 3:   Most Important Factors Influencing Internationalisation

Firm code	Most important	Second-most important	Third-most important
F1	Resources	Domestic competition	—
F2	Entrepreneurship	—	—
F3	Entrepreneurship	Business networks	Luck
F4	Seek opportunities	—	—
F5	Entrepreneurship	—	—
F6	Entrepreneurship	Resources	Business networks
F7	Entrepreneurship	—	—
F8	Entrepreneurship	—	—
F9	Domestic competition	Government policy	Entrepreneurship
F10	Entrepreneurship	Government policy	Market conditions
F11	Profit seeking	Government policy	—
F12	Government policy	Entrepreneurship	—
F13	Entrepreneurship	—	—
F14	Entrepreneurship	—	—
F15	Government policy	Entrepreneurship	—
F16	Entrepreneurship	Intern. Competition	—

Source: Wen and Liyun (2015, p. 203).

increasingly accessible to Chinese entrepreneurs. Another, over-stated and populist interpretation of this motivation is the desire to move capital out of China given the fear of political risk.

Liabilities of Foreignness

In his research, Rosch (2013) identifies the challenges, or liabilities of foreignness, that Chinese firms face, consistent with the biases discussed in Chapter 3 (Table 4).

Two challenges stand out: the discrimination hazard, at 22%, is consistent with the thesis on biases against Chinese firms, and the missing resources or capabilities hazard, at 43% is consistent with the thesis on Chinese firms lacking the necessary management capabilities. Consistent with Rosch, the KPMG/University of

Table 4:   Challenges for Chinese Firms' Foreign Investment

Challenge	Number of articles	% of total
Unfamiliarity hazards	11	48
Missing resources or capabilities	10	43
Discrimination hazards	5	22
Relational hazards	1	4
General	1	4
Not specified	6	26
Total	**23**	

Source: Rosch (2013, p. 56).

Sydney research highlights evidence of discrimination, including difficulty with institutional integration, such as working with trade unions (53% agree or strongly agree that it is difficult working with trade unions, whilst 45% were neutral to the proposition), and only 16% agree that Australian media are supportive of Chinese investment. On the proposition that Australia is more welcoming to investors from other countries than to Chinese investors, 50% agreed or strongly agreed, whilst 28% were neutral. Chinese investors felt that they were subject to unequal treatment and that their investment proposal should be evaluated on commercial criteria rather than ownership. The same research also provides evidence of the difficulty that Chinese firms experience in building good working relationships with local management: 62% answered either 'neutral' or 'disagree' that it is easy to build good relations with Australian executives, highlighting the difficulty in integrating foreign acquisitions and the complexity of cross-cultural management.

Rosch evaluates the strategies used by Chinese firms to cope with the liabilities of foreignness (Table 5).

The research shows a strong bias towards self-managing the internationalisation process, exploiting internal advantages, and leveraging external advantages (the latter two could be viewed as social network mechanisms), but it also highlights the challenges Chinese firms face in integrating into new markets. It also supports

Table 5:   **Strategies for Managing the Challenges of Foreign Investment**

Strategy	Number of articles	% of total
Managing the internationalisation process	16	74
Exploiting internal advantages	12	52
Leveraging external advantages	11	48
Leveraging human resource capabilities	5	21
Deploying marketing capabilities	4	17
Gaining legitimacy through isomorphism	1	4
Total	**23**	

Source: Rosch (2013, p. 57).

the hypothesis that Chinese firms prefer to encourage their own supply chains and networks to follow them.

International Management

The Four Cs framework highlights the importance of management competencies (proven, multi-disciplined management capabilities; the essential human capital critical to success in international markets). This is highly relevant, as the strategic decisions managements make inherently reflect their background and experience. In a Chinese context, Edward Tse (2015) notes that 'For those businesses seeking success abroad, it's not clear which of their China-developed skills will be relevant'.

The lack of essential management competencies was described by Wen and Liyun (2015: xii):

> When initiating international expansion, indigenous Chinese entrepreneurs are constrained by their low levels of education and experience and by unfavourable institutional arrangements, which results in their limited rationality … We argue that Chinese entrepreneurs have limited capabilities in assessing the degree of integration and homogeneity of the domestic and foreign markets and limited entrepreneurial cognition of international business opportunities.

Table 6: Importance of Experienced International Managers

Question	Very strongly agree (%)	Strongly agree (%)	Agree (%)	Neutral (%)	Disagree (%)	Strongly disagree (%)	Very strongly disagree (%)
International expansion is important to our firm's success	31	37	13	15		2	
Internationally experienced staff are important for our success in foreign markets	41	35	4	2		2	
Insufficient internationally experienced senior management is a constraint on our firm's growth strategy	26	28	26	13	6	2	
Senior management in each country must have experience in the local market	41	33	20	4			2

Source: Healy (2015). Dissertation Research. See Appendix 2.

Given this understandable qualification about the experience of Chinese management in international markets, the primary research explored this issue using 54 Chinese firms operating in Australia (Table 6).

The research provides a compelling picture on the importance of international expansion (80% strongly agree, very strongly agree, or agree). Interestingly, given the predicament facing Chinese firms, the findings support the importance of having experienced international managers (76% strongly agree or very strongly agree). The lack of internationally experienced staff, particularly staff with local market knowledge, is a constraint on international expansion (54% strongly agree or very strongly agree, and a further 26% agree), and the level of cross-cultural understanding and integration are important measures of how successfully Chinese firms can internationalise their operations and embrace cultural diversity. The findings show 64% strongly or very strongly agreeing that non-Chinese senior managers outside China must understand the Chinese market. Support is weaker when it comes to the need for international staff to have experience in China at HO (47% strongly or very strongly agree, and 26% are neutral). On the need for non-Chinese managers to understand Chinese culture, the evidence is very clear: 89% very strongly agree, strongly agree, or agree.

Summary

Whilst the international success of Chinese firms will depend greatly on the strength of their Four Cs, particularly their core capabilities, cultural adaptability, and the competencies of their management, there is little evidence that overseas expansion is based on these attributes. The strength of the Four Cs allows a first-mover advantage for Western firms, as their international organisational learning capability becomes an essential strategic asset, and, whilst strategic direction may change over time, a firm's 'administrative heritage' is less adaptable because it represents years of learning and development. Managerial competencies are important for building a firm's capabilities and can bestow a hard-to-replicate competitive advantage, but Chinese firms have a lot of catching up to do. To compensate for inherent weaknesses in some of the Four Cs, China's firms may benefit from a Fifth C — the cooperation of government, as described under the institutional theory. However, there is also much evidence that Chinese firms are following Deng's philosophy of expanding overseas without a blueprint and 'crossing the river by feeling for stones'.

The Four Cs theory of international strategy is one thing; succeeding with an international strategy is quite different. It is costly to confuse strategy with execution capabilities, a mistake made commonly by firms both in the West and in China. The early evidence of Chinese firms in the international arena highlights the capability gaps, together with poor execution discipline.

7

Firm Performance and the Role of the Financial System

The only boardrooms that shareholder value has not reached are those of China's state-run firms, whose CCP-appointed bosses look baffled if asked about return on capital and buzz for more tea.

The Economist

Internationalising a strategy is not a test of good management; good management understands that ultimately an international strategy can be justified only when it adds value greater than the opportunity cost of the capital and other resources employed domestically. Conventionally, firms are successful when they create sustainable value by earning an return on invested capital (ROIC) that is at least equal to their risk-adjusted cost of capital. Firms achieve this by having a firm-specific advantage (FSA) and proven execution capabilities, which allows them to grow their revenues and achieve a satisfactory ROIC. Firms that fail to achieve an ROIC at least equal to their risk-adjusted cost of capital operate at a loss in an economic sense regardless of their reported accounting-based profits; such firms return less to the economy than they use in resources, thus destroying wealth. If this occurs systemically across an industry or an economy, the long-term economic consequences can be profound. On the other hand, firms that create wealth for the owners are more likely to create value for other stakeholders and be more committed to corporate social responsibility, including their ability to invest and create new employment.

In the context of the internationalisation of Chinese firms, *The Economist* noted the following[1]:

> Chinese firms with little international experience and lots of debt have emerged as the biggest buyers of global assets … In recent years China has consistently accounted for less than a tenth of announced cross-border M&A deals; this year its share is nearly a third.

The Financial Times noted that there is a lengthening list of Chinese acquisitions that have turned sour, with about one quarter of all Chinese outbound deals, worth $270 billion between 2005 and 2015, having hit trouble. This, according to China expert Minxin Pei, Professor of Government at Claremont McKenna College in California, raises series concerns: 'People should ask whether such acquisitions are made with non-economic motives and whether China's acquirers have the capacity to manage these large, complex and innovative firms'. [2]

Creating sustainable value in foreign markets is challenging for any firm regardless of the country of origin. The costs associated with the liabilities of foreignness in entering foreign markets can result in underperformance and eventually market exit, as many Western firms will testify. The extent of these costs is defined by the nature of the market being entered and the transferable capabilities and other resources of the firm (the Four Cs). The additional costs can also be thought of as institutional and cultural differences between two countries and the problems that Western firms might face in working with Chinese firms. Another cost relates to the problems of information asymmetry. Chinese firms entering foreign markets through mergers and acquisitions (M&A) will know less about the acquired asset than the seller or better-informed domestic competitors. This problem was popularised by economist George

---

[1] *The Economist*, Money bags, April 2, 2016, pp. 61–63.
[2] *Financial Times*, M&A — China's world of debt, February 11, 2016.

Akerlof in his 'market for lemons' thesis. The essence of this 'lemon' problem is that poorly informed buyers of assets can overpay because they lack market knowledge and insights into the asset being sold, often combined with perfunctory due diligence. Akerlof illustrated this through the concept of *adverse selection*, in which buyers of assets meeting the seller's price might end up buying a 'lemon' instead of a 'peach'. High-quality assets, ('peaches') are rarely on the market. This problem is one which Chinese firms know well, as Professor Shambaugh (2012) notes:

> [Ninety] per cent of China's 300 overseas mergers and acquisitions conducted between 2008 and 2010 were unsuccessful, with Chinese companies losing 40–50 percent of their value after the acquisition.

Management inexperience aside (it is one thing to buy assets; it is another to execute well by integrating them and creating value), Chinese buyers are generally far more indebted than the firms they acquire. *The Economist* reported that, 'Of the deals announced since the start of 2015, the median debt-to-equity ratio of Chinese buyers has been 71 percent compared with 44 percent for the foreign targets'. When ChemChina offered $44 billion for Syngenta, the Swiss agrichemical giant in 2016, it had a total debt of 9.5 times its annual earnings before interest, tax, depreciation, and amortisation (EBITDA), putting it in the 'highly leveraged' category as defined by Standard and Poor's (S&P). The median debt to EBITDA multiple of the 54 Chinese firms that publish financial data and executed deals overseas in 2015 was 5.4 times, according to S&P Global Market Intelligence. Such a multiple would be regarded as 'highly leveraged' in sensibly functioning Western markets. Consistent with the Fifth C hypothesis (cooperation with government), much of the debt is provided by obliging Chinese banks, whose support for Chinese firms — many of whom, given their high level of financial leverage and weak profitability, would not be able to borrow from international banks — is encouraged by the CCP. Such a weak form of capital discipline adds to the unease with which Chinese overseas investment is seen, with undisciplined capital allocation by state-sponsored banks crowding out healthy private sector competition for assets and thereby distorting asset prices.

Whilst there was a genuine enthusiasm for making a profit in most Chinese firms, how that is achieved is not subject to the same execution discipline evident in well-managed firms in the West. As discussed below, factor productivity within Chinese firms is relatively poor, and challenging environments are not met with the same cost discipline seen in many Western firms. Moreover, investment and expansionary efforts tend not to adjust to prevailing environmental conditions. These responses partially reflect the differences in the national business system (NBS) experienced by Chinese managers, together with the influences of their own cultural heritage. Whilst commitment to making an accounting profit is serious, as shown in the KPMG/University of Sydney research (Appendix 3), many state-owned enterprises (SOEs) fail to break from their former selves.

Management Capabilities

The Four Cs emphasise the importance of capabilities of management. Research by Bloom *et al.* (2012) covering close to 10,000 firms across 20 countries, including China, highlighted the performance challenges faced by Chinese management (Table 1). The research rated 18 categories of management practices, which were then grouped into four broad categories by country: (i) overall management; (ii) monitoring of performance; (iii) management of performance targets; and (iv) management incentives aligned to performance outcomes.

All questions were rated 1 (low) to 5 (high), and the data relate to the manufacturing sector. Overall Management is the average score across all 18 questions. Each category of management practice reflects the average score, with both the highest and lowest scores for each category highlighted in bold. The ranking out of 20 countries for China by category is shown in brackets.

This research, which showed Chinese managers last or close to last in the four categories ranked, highlights the management challenge that Chinese firms face in improving productivity both

Table 1:   Management Quality Comparisons Across Countries

Country	Overall mgmt.	Monitoring mgmt.	Targets mgmt.	Incentive mgmt.	Firms interviewed
Argentina	2.76	3.08	2.67	2.56	246
Australia	3.02	3.27	3.02	2.75	392
Brazil	2.71	3.06	2.69	**2.55**	568
Canada	3.17	3.54	3.07	2.94	378
Chile	2.83	3.14	2.72	2.67	316
China	2.71(19)	**2.90**(20)	**2.62**(20)	2.69(15)	742
France	3.02	3.41	2.95	2.73	586
Germany	3.23	3.57	3.21	2.98	639
Greece	2.73	2.97	2.65	2.58	248
India	**2.67**	2.91	2.66	2.63	715
Italy	3.02	3.25	3.09	2.76	284
Japan	3.23	3.50	**3.34**	2.92	176
Mexico	2.92	3.29	2.89	2.71	188
New Zealand	2.93	3.18	2.96	2.63	106
Poland	2.90	3.12	2.94	2.83	350
Portugal	2.87	3.27	2.83	2.59	247
Rep. of Ireland	2.89	3.14	2.81	2.79	106
Sweden	3.20	**3.63**	3.18	2.83	382
UK	3.02	3.32	2.97	2.85	1214
US	**3.35**	3.57	3.25	**3.25**	1196
Average	2.99	3.28	2.94	2.82	9097

Source: Bloom *et al.* (2012); www.nber.org/papers/w17850.

domestically by implication and internationally by extrapolation. As noted in Chapter 8, Bloom *et al.* also indicate a strong correlation between the level of management education and survey ranking.

In another study of 30 privately-owned enterprise (POEs), Hout and Michael (2014) found that most firms displayed a trading mentality that emphasised timing over perfection; they also exhibited a Confucian preference for hierarchical organisation structure and a deep fear of instability linked to China's experience, together with well-honed skills in managing different levels of government.

Real Profit, Not Accounting Profit: Shareholder Value

Whilst the concept of 'shareholder value' has been discredited in the minds of many and is often associated with CEO greed, short-termism, underinvestment, corporate scandals, and societal inequality (Enron, for example, pledged to 'create significant value for our shareholders', Lehman Bros. prioritised 'maximising shareholder value', and WorldCom had a 'proven record of shareholder value creation'), it remains one of the most influential ideas in business and represents a philosophy that is understood and practised by the best-managed firms in the world, including some Chinese firms. *The Economist* noted the following[3]:

> Outbreaks of madness in markets tend to happen because people are breaking the rules of shareholder value, not enacting them ... That such fiascos occur is a failure of governance and human nature, not an idea ... Fosun a private Chinese firm, devotes a page of its annual report to calculating the value it claims to have created.

The gap in performance between China's SOEs and POEs was documented by Lardy (2014) and the McKinsey Global Institute, who calculate that POEs made a 12% return on assets in 2015 compared to only 4% by SOEs. The management challenge and productivity opportunity in China was also evaluated by the McKinsey Global Institute (2016), who calculated that 80% of all 'economic profit' (profit after the cost of capital is charged, thus a measure of whether shareholder value is being created) comes from the finance industry, reflecting the privileges afforded and the regulatory protection given to state-owned banks. Using economic profit as a measure, almost half of the 20 biggest Chinese industries take a loss.

Economic Profit More Important than Accounting Profit

Because the financial reporting framework is based on accounting rather than economic principles, it can give an impression

---

[3] *The Economist*, Analyse this, April 2, 2016, pp. 58–59.

Table 2: Simple Comparison between Accounting and Economic Profit

	Firm A	Firm B
Revenue	$5,000	$5,000
Net operating profit after tax (NOPAT)	$500	$600
NOPAT margin	10%	12%
Capital employed	$4,000	$6,500
Capital charge @ 10%	$400	$650
Economic profit	$100	($50)

about performance that is misleading. It is not unusual for management to treat a range of expense items such as write-offs or restructuring charges as 'exceptional items' that they argue should be ignored when assessing performance. It is common for assets to be written-off, which is an admission that previous investment decisions were wrong, but it is not uncommon for management incentives to be based on 'underlying performance' even though shareholder outcomes are determined *after* so-called 'exceptional items'. The biggest flaw in the accounting model is that it implicitly assumes that equity capital is free and should not be paid for, even though investors need a return to compensate for risk.

An economic profit measure addresses these inconsistencies by focusing on the profit from operations and then deducting a cost for the capital employed in the firm (debt and equity).

This example highlights an important concept at the heart of shareholder value and good management: an economic profit is made only when the cost of capital (debt and equity) provided to the firm is at least covered. In Table 2, Firms A and B have the same revenue, but Firm B makes more net operating profit after tax (NOPAT). However, Firm B consumes more capital ($6,500) than Firm B ($4,000). Thus, when the cost of that capital is charged at a rate of 10%, Firm A makes an economic profit of $100, whilst Firm B takes a loss of $50. Firm B destroys value, even though it makes a higher accounting profit. The traditional accounting profit implicitly assumes that the cost of equity capital is free, whereas investors providing equity require a return in line with the risk-adjusted opportunity cost of equity.

The Economic Profit formula is

$$\text{Economic Profit} = \text{NOPAT} - \text{Cost of Capital}$$

or

$$\text{ROIC} - \text{Cost of Capital} = \text{Economic Profit}$$

Another way to think about ROIC and economic profit is through the lens of factor productivity. In China, the McKinsey & Co. study demonstrates that the productivity of Chinese firms has generally been poor, with labour productivity running at 15–30% of the OECD average. *The Economist*,[4] reporting on the McKinsey Global Institute study, commented that a comparative analysis of 10,000 Chinese and American firms showed that 75% of the difference in the performance gap is explained by the performance of individual firms — of management — rather than industry conditions (*Businesses do not fail, it's management that fails*). This is an important finding.

The same McKinsey & Co. study revealed that Chinese firms are consuming 60% more capital to produce one unit of GDP growth compared to the 1990–2010 levels. This has meant that profitability has been neglected in many Chinese firms, particularly the SOEs, who can act in a manner that emphasises principal–agent problems (agency costs), or, to use an old Chinese saying, 'the mountains are high and the emperor is far away'. In other words, many SOEs give lip service to their ultimate masters, and, absent effective market disciplines, are largely free to do so. In a bank-dominant financial system, the banks should play a critical role in monitoring for agency costs, including unproductive investments.

---

[4] *The Economist*, Sleepy giant — China Inc. needs better management, June 25, 2016, p. 54.

The Critical Role of Banks

To understand the strength and potential of any economy, the relation between the financial system and investment decisions is pivotal; this is also highly relevant to understanding the strengths and weaknesses of the Chinese economy. The structure and development of an efficient financial market and financial institutions stimulates both savings and productive investment, thereby driving economic growth. These are universal truths. The concept of a financial system is defined by the combination of financial markets and financial institutions. In a bank-dominated financial system, the banks' effectiveness in allocating capital can play an important role in the productivity of that economy, avoiding or creating the financial instability risk described by Minsky (Chapter 3) and the inherent macroeconomic risks in the economy created by, for example, asset bubbles caused by reckless lending and asset-class concentration. The Chinese financial system can be described as deep but narrow, in that it is a system dominated by banks (Naughton, 2006). Though other forms of financial institutions have emerged, their impact has not been meaningful, aside from the so-called 'shadow banking system', though, as noted earlier, China leads the world in the growth of fintechs. The Asian financial crisis of 1997–1998 highlighted the risks of rapidly growing economies with underdeveloped and narrowly based financial systems.

Stepping into theory for a moment is helpful in building a complete picture of the challenges facing Chinese banks and policymakers. Two defining books were written in 1973, one by R.I. McKinnon, *Money and Capital Development*, and another by E.S. Shaw, *Financial Deepening in Economic Development*. These books developed a powerful theory that assists an understanding of the Chinese financial system, particularly the link between finance and investment through the Financial Liberalisation Model (FLM), which looks at the central role of interest rates and quantitative constraints such as credit rationing by commercial banks. Financial liberalisation policies are designed to reform a country's financial system by acting on a few key variables and regulations and have powerful effects on institutions and markets. Since financial liberalisation policies are designed to change the financial system, a useful question in the Chinese context is 'from what to what?'

The McKinnon–Shaw concept of the FLM assumes that financial systems work well if flows of credit and stocks of financial assets are determined by efficiently and freely operating financial markets. Thus, market efficiency ensures that the price of borrowing and lending decisions operate within free markets that achieve an equilibrium. A repressed financial system is one in which markets are prevented from working well; obstacles prevent the prices of financial assets from being at their equilibrium values. The critical assumption, which holds true in China, is that commercial banks are the main financial institutions in the financial system and that bank deposits are the main financial assets.

The obstacles can affect many financial variables and can originate from many causes, but the standard version of the McKinnon–Shaw model concentrates upon one financial variable and one cause relevant to China. The financial variable that is prevented from being in equilibrium is interest rates on bank deposits, and the cause of that repression is government policy that prevents banks from adjusting interest rates upwards to equilibrium. The result is a form of credit rationing and subsidisation from the household sector to (primarily) SOEs, which, given government intervention, causes finance to be allocated to inefficient investment projects. The negative consequences of this form of financial repression comes at the cost to GDP growth, which could be estimated in the order of 3–5% pa before counting the costs of a policy framework that prevents meaningful competition, including creating a level playing field in which foreign banks can freely operate.

Central to a bank-dominated financial system is the asymmetric information problem, in which borrowers know more about the risk in their business than lenders do. This creates the problem of adverse selection, whereby borrowers seeking assets for growth accept risky projects that may or are likely to result in adverse outcomes. A related theme is moral hazard, whereby borrowers, with the advantage of superior information, are likely to engage in risky projects, believing that banks will accommodate contract adjustments in the event of financial distress, a phenomenon common in China. In part, the latter is mitigated by the effectiveness of the *monitoring* role played by the bank as a lender. To do this, however, banks must be independent and act commercially in allocating capital, pricing risk and monitoring performance to manage their risk.

In theory, banks should act as intermediary depositors and borrowers, ensuring an efficient allocation of capital to well-managed firms and households to allow for investment and safeguard depositor funds. The investment and monitoring role that banks play is critical to a vibrant economy; underpinning this is the principle that banks should lend only according to commercial principles, founded on sound risk management. The theory on banking is one thing; the practice of banking in China is often viewed as quite another thing. Critics point to a system that lacks a real credit culture or risk management skills and that continues to pour money into value-destroying activities, creating a huge risk to the entire financial system and broader economy, with contagion risk for international markets. The high level of indebtedness of many SOEs and high-profile POEs created a practice of 'evergreen loans', which, when they become delinquent, are simply restructured into a new loan or swapped from debt-to-equity to alleviate their burden. Moreover, as discussed in Chapter 4, the banks play a central role in China's chequebook diplomacy, including extending credit to nations, such as Laos and Venezuela, with a high risk of default. As noted in Chapter 3, McKinsey & Co. suggest that the ratio of nonperforming loans within the banking system in 2015 was closer to 7% than the officially reported 1.7%.

In China, the political involvement in bank lending is a flawed characteristic of the repressed financial system, adding avoidable costs to the economy. Any move to insist that banks operate on purely commercial lines has met with resistance from local CCP officials (the dukes), who see their influence over how capital is allocated as a powerful and important instrument of their authority. All of this supports the thesis that Chinese firms enjoy a Fifth C in the form of cooperation with government, as is evident, for example, in the high leverage in some of the M&A deals mentioned above.

The Chinese financial system, particularly the banking system, may prove to be the Achilles' heel of the economy, representing a significant concern for policymakers in other markets, particularly those where highly leveraged Chinese firms have made acquisitions. The failure of a Chinese firm due to indebtedness could have a contagion effect across an industry in the economy in which the Chinese-owned firm operates.

8

Management Education

The mechanic, who wishes to do his work well, must first sharpen his tools.

Confucius

That management education is a driver of firm and economic performance is a generally accepted truth and is evident by the growth in investment in business-related higher education and by the number of Western senior executives who hold higher business degrees or have attended an executive development programme. This reflects a belief that successful international leaders and managers are not born but develop through education and experience. Bloom *et al.* (2012) demonstrated in their research of 10,000 firms across 20 countries, which, as discussed in Chapter 7, showed that the level of education of managers is 'strongly linked to better management practices' and that firms that use the most widely accepted management techniques, of the type taught at business school, outperform their peers. In a Harvard Business Review (HBR) article Sadun *et al.* (2017) reaffirmed earlier research: 'our data shows that the average management score (capability) is significantly higher at firms with better-educated employees'. In their research on the internationalisation of firms, Alon *et al.* (2013), also highlighted the link between education and the development of international strategies.

The central premise of management education is that it equips individuals with essential multidisciplinary knowledge and can help

135

develop the leadership and management competencies needed to successfully manage businesses in a dynamic global environment. Bloom *et al.* (2012: 17) observe the following:

> Our belief is that more basic education — for example, around capital budgeting, data analysis and standard human resources practices — could help improve management in many countries. This holds particularly true in developing countries.

The emphasis on management education is not to argue that all successful business leaders have to attain a formal business education, even though professionals such as doctors, lawyers, engineers, and accountants must meet formal education standards in order to practice their profession (but, ironically given the ethical and trust issues facing banks, bankers do not).[1] The extent to which management should be considered a distinct profession subject to formal education is not universally agreed upon. The president of Harvard University in the first edition of the HBR in 1923 wrote about 'The Profession of Business' and the need to see business as a distinct profession (Barker, 2010). The following three articles in the HBR in recent years highlight the divergence of views: (i) *Management Is Not a Profession — But It Can Be Taught*; (ii) *It's Time to Make Management a True Profession*; and (iii) *Why Management Must Be a Profession*. Harvard Business School professors Khurana and Nohria (2008) argue the case for regarding management as a true profession. The contrary view is argued by Mintzberg (2004: 1), who writes that 'Management is a practice that has to blend a good deal of craft (experience) with a certain amount of art (insight) and some science (analysis)'.

Mintzberg's view on the craft of management is challenged by a growing view that the underlying practice and study of management and business lends its self to science and that decision-making should rely on scientific analysis, such algorithmic-driven risk decisioning over human judgement in banking, for example. The explosion of and emphasis on big data and growing interest in

---

[1] The author is a member of the Chartered Institute of Bankers (Scotland).

Artificial Intelligence (AI) reinforce this idea. In a survey of senior executives by EY in the US, (Martin and Golsby-Smith, 2017), 81% of executives said that 'data should be at the heart of all decision-making', which lead EY to proclaim, 'big data can eliminate the reliance on 'gut feel' decision-making'. This emphasis on science is underlined by the growing priority given in MBA programmes to strengthen the notion that management can be practiced as a hard science. But is it true that management is a science? If true, what role does relationship building, imagination, bold transformative thinking, inspirational leadership, communication and behavioural traits play? In their excellent book *Nudge* (2008), Professors Thaler and Sustien (2008) show how behavioural factors influence decision-making in ways that may not seem rational. In his excellent book, *Irrational Exuberance*, Professor Shiller(2000) shows how perfectly rational and sophisticated financial markets' professionals can and do behave in an irrational manner, ignoring all warnings of impending risk. There is much evidence to support the growing field on behavioural economics as an important lens in understanding decision-making in business and politics. Given the predisposition of Chinese education to hard sciences such as engineering and computing, there is a risk that the emphasis on management as a science will dominate Chinese management. Science has an important role to play in management decisioning, but it shouldn't be overstated.

What is not in dispute is that management education is now a fast-growing business with over 1,200 institutions around the world offering management education; this excludes the growth in 'corporate universities' such as McDonald's University. In 2013–2014, US universities awarded 189,000 Master's degrees in business,[2] compared to 50,000 MBAs graduating from Chinese universities.[3] In the US, 11.7 million applications are made to business schools annually for places on master-level degrees in business, with the top schools receiving 150–200 applications for every available place.[4]

---

[2] *The Economist*, Campus versus beach, October 15, 2016, p. 58.
[3] *The Economist*, The World in 2017, p. 117.
[4] *The Financial Times*, Changing course: A harder sell for MBAs, October 22, 2016.

The creation of management schools in Europe and North America in the late 19th century and the first half of the 20th century led to a greater degree of standardisation and systemisation of understanding on the importance of management knowledge and techniques. The Wharton Business School at the University of Pennsylvania was founded in 1881, and the first graduate school of business in the US, the Tuck School of Business at Dartmouth College, was established in 1900. Harvard Business School was founded in 1908, and Europe's first business school, ESCP in Paris, was founded in 1819. The first Chinese business school, CEIBS, was established in 1994. Many scholars (e.g. Wang, He, and Yu, 2005: 165) argue that the field of education management is unique and should be differentiated from fields such as law, engineering, and medicine because the nature of knowledge in management is subjective, contextual, and multidisciplinary rather than objectively based on universal truths. Therefore, case study and reflection-based learning is prevalent, with 'no right or wrong' answers. This perspective on management education and the lack of universally agreed professional standards adds to the difficulty in clearly defining why it is important for managers to achieve accreditation in the way that lawyers, engineers, or doctors must. Management requires adaptive skills and a multidisciplinary approach, whereas lawyers will focus on issues legal and doctors on matters medical. Barker (2010) summarised the dilemma facing management education by referencing feedback from corporate leaders on the MBA program at London Business School (LBS):

> Corporate leaders produced an extensive list of qualities they desired in future recruits, but almost none involved functional or technical knowledge. Rather, virtually all their requirements could be summed as follows: the need for more thoughtful, more aware, more sensitive, more flexible, more adaptive managers capable of being moulded and developed into global executives.

These are attributes rather than skills and are highly subjective. It would be wrong to conclude that technical skills are not important, as the LBS survey might suggest. Rather, technical skills can be viewed as core foundation skills, abundant in the English-speaking West, which are necessary but not sufficient in a well-rounded international manager, who must be competent in integrating across a range of disciplines and be culturally astute. The demands placed on management knowledge and education can be relatively straightforward if a firm limits its activities to a well-known domestic market and product range. The tools needed to succeed in an internationally competitive and complex world are very different.[5] International managers have to develop a global mindset, have access to relevant knowledge, and, in addition to having a high intelligence quotient (IQ), they must also develop a sophisticated culturally-adept emotional quotient (EQ). In the Chinese context, there is also much emphasis on a manager's need to have a high spiritual quotient (SQ) — the ability to understand that people have a need for meaning and a sense of worth in what they do.

Contemporary international business leaders must also be well-versed in ethics, given the scrutiny exerted by policymakers, opinion leaders, and the media. Whilst business ethics has grown in prominence in management education, particularly after the GFC, where it is no longer an optional elective at the best schools, it remains underemphasised in China, as Song (2005: 67) comments: 'some visiting western academics admit privately that lecturing to Chinese business students about ethics is greeted by apathy', given a natural tendency towards scientific reasoning.

The challenge for management education worldwide has been an erosion in confidence in MBA (and equivalent) qualifications,

---

[5] The author has deep experience of this, which includes working for a major US bank in London, where in a highly culturally diverse environment, there was a deep global view on business, in contrast to working with an Australian bank whose management horizons rarely extended beyond Melbourne and Sydney. The author has also experienced a hybrid of these extremes in working for another Australian bank which had a strong internationally experienced senior management who had populated the bank with international bankers. The difference in perspective in all three institutions provides is evidence of the hypothesis that institutions are shaped by senior management backgrounds.

particularly its relevance given the demands of the modern global economy. At the same time, business schools have been criticised for the role they played in creating the conditions that led to the GFC, including (until then) the lack of emphasis on ethics and corporate social responsibility. Many argue that the value proposition that once made management education an essential qualification for aspiring business leaders is no longer clear. Though business schools are among the acknowledged successes of higher education, there are growing questions about their value, ability to adapt, relevance, and future. The growth of online MBAs and other business-related Master's degrees is a response to a demand from a more technology-literate market, many of whom have known only a digital world and want an online offering.

In assessing the value of management education in the degree form, a core question is, 'Do business schools produce better managers?' In management education, much emphasis is placed on MBA programmes (and equivalents), which Mintzberg criticises (Mintzberg, 2004). He argues that 'business education' distorts management practice, rather than developing managers in a serious educational process:

> Too much of a disconnect between the practice of management and what was being taught in classrooms, with most current programmes over-emphasise domain knowledge and underemphasise the multi-disciplinary nature of management.

Mintzberg is not arguing that management education should occur outside the academia; his analysis shows that more great ideas that have shaped business practice have come from the academia than from consultants or business (e.g. Michael Porter's work on competition, industry structure, and competitive advantage, and the Black–Scholes options pricing model developed by Fischer Black and Myron Scholes, which revolutionised finance). He is arguing that the current approach lacks relevance and is flawed. Globally, business education is at a crossroads, with critics arguing that MBA programmes fail to give students essential leadership, decision-making skills, cultural awareness, and a global perspective, which are critical to success. Instead, critics argue, business schools are churning out skilled analysts.

Management Education in China

In 1917, China's first management class was taught at Fudan University in Shanghai. War and the rise of the CCP saw management education all but vanish until the 1990s. Up until the 1980s, under the planned economy, there was little demand or incentive for professionally trained managers. For political and ideological reasons, management education had been disregarded. It was only with the reforms and opening up that management education as it was taught in the West reappeared, and the Chinese government came to understand its importance.

This vacuum that emerged post-1949 was exaggerated by the chaos of the Cultural Revolution, resulting in a lost generation of intellectual input for management practices. The generation that should represent the senior leaders and mentors to the younger generation today were denied a formal education during the Cultural Revolution. Mao Zedong categorised intellectuals as the 'stinking ninth category' on his list of 'nine black categories' in Chinese society. When business schools were beginning to flourish in the West, the Chinese education system was being restructured along Soviet lines, which meant giving priority to practical subjects such as engineering and natural sciences and dismantling liberal education. Following several 1,000 years of tradition, Chinese pedagogy emphasises rote learning and memorisation, encouraging homogeneity and standardisation. Not surprisingly, there were many critics of a system where teaching methods are passive, with a one-way delivery of lectures and test-paper examinations that deliver a process of recalling what is in the textbook. Lectures are often based on information from textbooks with limited practical value and an emphasis on the 'correct answer'. In many ways, the convergence of Confucian and Leninist models of management thinking presents challenges for free and open critical inquiry. The emphasis on ensuring compliance with Party ideology, threatens those who seek to explore ideas that may be viewed as 'harmful'. The CCP issued a communique in 2013 to all universities, providing a list of 'Seven Prohibitions' governing university teaching and research. The communique clearly spelt out that academics who tolerate 'the illegal spread of harmful ideas and expressions in the classroom will be dealt with severely according to regulation and law'. The long shadow of the CCP casts itself over university teaching and the market for ideas and critical thought. Chinese learning also tends to neglect the art of hypothesis formulation and the development of problem-solving skills, much needed in a volatile business environment, in favour of rote learning. Some evidence of the contrast in philosophy was highlighted by reports that the University of Sydney had failed a disproportionate number of Chinese on critical thinking business skills.[6]

The resultant gap in management capabilities was highlighted in a McKinsey & Co survey in which HR professionals at multinational firms were asked to evaluate Chinese graduates. The survey revealed that 85% were unsuited to work in an international setting for three critical reasons: excessive reliance on rote learning, poor English, and low mobility (Beardson, 2014).

However, demand for management education has increased since China's entry to the WTO, with business schools like the Shanghai-based China Europe International Business School (Ceibs) flourishing (Ceibs was ranked 11th best business school in the world by the *Financial Times* business school ranking in 2017, up from 17th in 2016).[7] Cultural problems in adopting Western-style education remain, even though management education is a core competency of many Western universities. Reflecting a growing trend in Western business schools partnering with Chinese universities, the Dean of the School of Management at Fudan University commented that[8]

---

[6] Sydney University denies allegations of deliberately failing Chinese students (www.abc.net.au/news/2015-08-06/university..students), and other Australian universities are accused of deliberately failing Chinese students (shanghaiist. com/2015/08/08/Australian_university_accused).

[7] *Financial Times*, China's roving students are lured home, September 25, 2017.

[8] *Financial Times*, Business school to open in Kuala Lumpur, April 20, 2015.

'Management education in China had just taken off and there was an urgent need for introducing advanced theory and methodology from Western countries'. On the relevance of adapting Western education to Chinese conditions, Lamb and Currie (2012) in their research suggest that the power of market logic has 'eclipsed the normative calls for adaptation', resulting in the adoption of the 'US MBA model'. However, others argue that China cannot depend on the West to develop a suitable management education model and must develop its own indigenous model, blending the best of both East and West. Li *et al.* (2005: 13) echo these sentiments:

> There is a dire need to elaborate effective pedagogies for future management leaders of the Greater China economy. It appears that most business and management education in the Greater China region simply borrow pedagogies and methodologies from the Western countries. While these may be useful approaches, cultural, work and societal and economic system differences are often given short shrift.

The growing chorus demanding a Chinese-specific or Asian model of management education is loud, arguing that the case for a region-specific theory of management education is a 'patent need' and that a 'theoretical understandings developed in one setting may not work in another'. Customising Western education models to meet Chinese needs, at a minimum, requires overlaying cultural values.

Research Findings

In the primary research, the issues around management education (ME) and its relevance to internationally focused Chinese firms was explored (Table 1).

The findings reveal strong support for the importance of management education to a firm's international strategy (64% strongly or very strongly agree; a further 33% agree) and for building the management capabilities needed for success in international markets (51% strongly or very strongly agree; a further 46% agree). The importance of cross-cultural understanding is strongly supported

Table 1:   Relevance of Management Education (ME)

Question	Very strongly agree (%)	Strongly agree (%)	Agree (%)	Neutral (%)	Disagree (%)	Strongly disagree (%)	Very strongly disagree (%)
ME is important to our international strategy	31	33	33	2			
ME is important in building management capabilities needed to succeed overseas	18	33	46		2		
Cross-cultural management is important to our firms international strategy	30	41	28	2			
MBA qualified executives will be preferred in international appointments	11	13	26	37	13		
ME with 'Chinese characteristics' is important to the development of management talent	7	17	39	22	13		
In hiring young executives, formal ME is preferred	13	24	43	9	11		

(*Continued*)

Table 1: (*Continued*)

Question	Very strongly agree (%)	Strongly agree (%)	Agree (%)	Neutral (%)	Disagree (%)	Strongly disagree (%)	Very strongly disagree (%)
Management training within the business is preferred to external programs	11	19	41	24	9		
Difficult to assess the value of the investment in ME	3		43	19	35		
ME is too theoretical and not relevant to business needs	2	2	30	26	39	2	
Highly educated executives are difficult to retain	4	11	31	28	24	2	

Source: Healy (2015).

(71% strongly or very strongly agree, and 28% agree), highlighting its importance in management education.

Summary

The research findings on the relevance of the traditional MBA programme are mixed. Whilst 80% of respondents agree, strongly agree, or very strongly agree that, in hiring young executives, formal management education is preferred, but support for MBA (or equivalent) training is not as profound. There is a preference for in-house training, whilst there is a balance on the question of how management education should be valued, with 43% agreeing that it is difficult to value, 35% disagreeing, and 19% remaining neutral. The questioning on the value of MBAs (and equivalents) should not be confused with the importance placed on management education, with a rejection of the view that management education is too theoretical, not grounded in business, and has a value that is difficult to assess. Several respondents emphasised that a tailor-made programme related to the challenges of the business is key, a trend evident in the data, with 30% strongly or very strongly agreeing on a preference for internal programmes and a further 41% agreeing. One respondent summed the situation up as follows:

> Management education should be tailored to help management understand the complexity in cultural diversity and the importance in today's business world for international firms. This will be the foundation for the success of the firm's international venture.

Another respondent commented as follows:

> I strongly agree that management education is essential for any company with an ambition for the future, but a customised education program is the key so that the needs of the company are an important factor.

The view that Chinese firms seek management education with 'Chinese characteristics' is generally but not emphatically supported (25% strongly or very strongly agree; a further 39% agree). As with the literature, the weight of opinion seems balanced, and the extent to which Chinese characteristics replace or augment Western-based management education is a question of degree. It is an important theme, however, given the criticality of two of the Four Cs — competency of management and cultural adaptability — in determining success in the global economy and how these Cs help build FSA. Hamel and Prahalad (1996) are quoted in Chapter 6 and are presented again given their significance:

Management will be judged on how well they identify, cultivate and exploit core competencies that will make sustainable growth possible. Core competencies are the collective learning of an organisation; cultivating core competencies is the best way to prevail in global competition.

The research findings from Bloom *et al.* (2012) provide measurement values for a generally accepted truth — that management education can make a crucial difference to how firms perform and to how economies develop.

9

Concluding Remarks

If companies do not globalise, China won't become powerful.

Wang Jianlin, Chairman, Dalian Wanda

Given the size of the Chinese economy and the emergence of firms like Alibaba, HNA, Fusan, Huawei, and many others, it seems inevitable that Chinese firms will play a major role in the global economy, including being an active player in cross-border M&A, well into the future. What we have seen to date is the appetiser, not the main dish. Whilst there has been 33% pa growth in Chinese Outbound Foreign Direct Investment (OFDI) in the 5 years leading up to 2016, Chinese firms spent only 0.9% of GDP on outbound M&A, compared to the 2% spent by European firms and the 1.3% of GDP spent by US firms (McKinsey & Co., 2017). Moreover, the stock of China's outbound investment is small compared to many Western nations at less than one-tenth of the stock of overseas investment of the UK or Europe and less than one-twentieth of the US, whose stock of OFDI exceeds $5 trillion. China's stock of OFDI as a proportion of GDP stands at close to 8%, compared to 38% for the US, 20% for Japan, 47% for Germany, and 32% for Australia. By any measure, Chinese firms have a significant growth runway in front of them if they are to catch up with the global presence of firms from the major developed nations. The One Belt, One Road (OBOR) strategy will act as one channel of growth, but so will cross-border M&A particularly into Western Europe, Australia, and the US.

China is unique. Given the unavoidable political and geopolitical context, the sheer scale of the internationalisation of Chinese firms warrants analysis of its form and motives. Positioned within a broad context, this book is about the ability of Chinese firms to successfully internationalise their operations, with an emphasis on the Four C's framework. A central argument in this book is that the success of Chinese firms in the international economy cannot be separated from China's unique and complex socioeconomic, cultural, political, and geopolitical context; hence, the evidence of a compensatory Fifth C. The history of China and the richness of Confucian values are relevant when considering the strategic decisions managements make, which inherently reflect their background and experience. As Henry Kissinger (2011) reminded us, a common cultural trait of the Chinese leadership was their emphasis on an historical perspective; he also reminds us that history is to a country what character is to people.

Following the lead from a globally astute President Xi, the new generation of emerging Chinese managers is much better versed in Western practices, the attractions of the international economy, and the capability of borderless social networks and technology to create opportunities. They are also deeply nationalistic and patriotic, as they should be. The Century of Humiliation is never to be forgotten, as the Chinese education system goes to great lengths to emphasise. The power to pull on the heart strings of 'the motherland' is no different for the Chinese than for the diaspora from other nations, religions, or races. Australia and the US know this well. This is natural and should not cause conflicts, though some might feel uncomfortable when Chinese students and residents in Australia, for example, rally for issues when the Chinese embassy cajoles for support, as many in the Jewish community, for example, might rally around matters important to Israel. With more than 50 million ethnic Chinese living outside China, forming the world's largest diaspora, the power of national patriotism was understood by President Xi, when he said in a 2014 speech that 'Generations of overseas Chinese never forget their home country, their origins or the blood of the Chinese nation flowing in their veins'.[1] Indeed, the goal of the 'great rejuvenation of

---

[1] *The Economist*, Who is Chinese? The upper Han, November 19, 2016.

the Chinese nation' (*Zhonghua minzu weida fuxing*) can be interpreted as embracing the 'Chinese race' — including anyone with Chinese blood anywhere in the world *(Zhonghua minzu)*. Premier Li Keqiang emphasised this: 'The Chinese race is a big family and feelings of love for the motherland, passion for the homeland, are infused in the blood of every single person with Chinese ancestry'.[2]

Linked to the Chinese diaspora and the growing internationalisation of its firms, lingering in the background in shaping Western views on China is the question of China's geopolitical ambitions. Does it want to *dominate the world?* as Jonathan Fenby (2016) asks. Those interested in geopolitical history will know that the idea of a new power displacing existing hegemons is not new, as the Thucydides's Trap thesis shows. As Professor Allison (2017) reminds us, the propensity for this to end in war is uncomfortably high given historical precedents. The evidence of any hostility in the ambitions of Chinese leaders is scant, however. Global ambitions in trade and investment are clearly enunciated, but China's global military, diplomatic, cultural, and soft power footprint is miniscule compared to its economic might. For example, outside China, Chinese is not nearly as widespread a method of communication as English, Spanish, or Arabic is. However, history also tells us that major wars can result from accidents rather than through specific intent; in other words, nations can inadvertently stumble into a major conflict. The law of unintended consequence can result in unplanned outcomes.

Given the Thucydides' Trap hypothesis, the world faces a dilemma agreeing on a policy framework for managing affairs with China and Chinese firms. This is particularly evident in Australia, with its historical allegiance to the US. Hugh White of the Australian National University commented that Australia has 'subcontracted its entire strategic role (in Asia) to Washington' whilst warning that Australia must prepare for a China-led future.[3] As do many other Western and Asian nations, Australia grapples with how to have China as a friend and avoid having it as an enemy. No country wants to get on the wrong side of its biggest customer. Whilst most nations

---

[2] *Financial Times*, The dark side of China's national renewal, June 21, 2017.
[3] *The Economist*, Asian geopolitics, April 22, 2017.

welcome the opportunity to grow trade and capital flows with China, there is a niggling uncertainty about the consequences of becoming too beholden, and clear thinking is clouded by a mix of a blinkered approach, a mist of 'red-phobia', and anti-China myopia. Good old-fashioned biases, conscious and unconscious, easily control the mindset. There is no getting away from the reality that China and Chinese firms face major image problems around the world, but how much of this is based on a realisation that China, with a clear long-term strategy and leadership stability, is on ascendancy whilst the West (and many of its institutions), with no apparent strategy, is facing a crisis of identity? The hot breath of this economic dragon can be felt on the backs of many in the West. Former Australian PM, Kevin Rudd, captured this succinctly when he wrote: 'The West needs to reflect on its own condition. Since the fall of the Soviet Union there has been little strategic direction about the idea of the west itself, and the core elements of the liberal democratic and capitalist project. Instead, the west is increasingly self-absorbed, self-satisfied and globally complacent. China is marching towards its perception of its global destiny. It has a strategy. The West has none'.[4]

Critics of China's state-owned enterprises (SOEs) and privately-owned enterprises (POEs) buying of assets in foreign markets point to the CCP's '*go global*' directive and the opaque nature of ownership structures, lack of transparency around decision-making, unstable financing structures, and the absence of Western-style corporate governance, all creating a sense that business goals are not framed in conventional commercial ways. Lingering behind this suspicion is a sense that the invisible-hand (and often the visible hand) of the CCP is at play, creating a level of political risk that could impact Chinese investments in foreign markets, and thus the industries and economies in those markets. Business and political leaders in the West see the CCP as having significant influence and sometimes ultimate control over Chinese firms — SOEs and POEs alike — and can be unpredictable (*signal left, but turn right*), whereas firms in the West are

---

[4] *Financial Times*, Xi Jinping offers a long-term view of China's ambition, October 23, 2017.

free to pursue their profit-seeking goals, subject to clearly enunciated laws, regulations, and well-understood motivations. This is true to a point, but it would be misleading to state that government and business in the West are entirely separate; there is overwhelming evidence on the powerful role that big business plays in policymaking and the propensity, in an age of populism, for Western governments to interfere in the conduct of business and markets. It is not also unusual for senior politicians to find second careers in 'big business' where the perception of conflicts of interest can be conveniently ignored. It is also true that the social license granted to 'big business' and in Australia, the major banks, is open to democratic review.

The political environment in the West is increasingly beholden to populist views, which often trump rational logic. Witness, for example, the decision by the Ford Motor Company following the election of President Trump to cancel its planned $1.6 billion investment in Mexico and reassign the investment commitment to the US. There is strong evidence that Chinese firms can be subject to 'national interest' vetoes on their investment plans, whereas other cross-border transactions can go by without a murmur of official disapproval, as was evident when Softbank, a Japanese firm, acquired the UK's most successful technology firm, ARM, for $31 billion in 2016. The media play a pivotal role in creating anxiety by, amongst other things, perpetrating the myth that China is 'buying the world', whereas the clear evidence demonstrates the contrary. As Nolan (2012) notes, 'the West is inside China, but China is not inside the West', and giant Western-based 'systems integrators' dominate the global economy. These are some of the practical realities facing Chinese firms in trying to operate in the global economy, all combining to present insurmountable challenges that can be described as the *five biases*.

When it comes to financial economics and strategy, this book argues that universal principles apply and there is no substantive case for developing a different set of rules or theories for Chinese firms. Mainstream strategy theory centred on a resource-based view of the firm is challenged in explaining the internationalisation of Chinese firms. Given the rapid pace of internationalisation, it should be no surprise that the growth in OFDI has outstripped the labour market's capacity to produce the necessary quantity of trained and experienced Chinese managers. Few would dispute that China has a lot of catching up to do in developing *human capital* including management talent and that the lack of experienced and skilled management is a constraint on firms as they compete in international markets and manage what they have acquired. Whilst much progress has been made in improving technical management skills and a new generation of Chinese managers is emerging, there remains a dearth of experience in executing M&A in international markets. This is not a capability that can be taught simply through a course of study at business school or that lends itself to a 'silver bullet' solution. Experience and practical knowledge matter on a foundation of sound business and economic theory. Only through experience can Chinese firms familiarise themselves with the 'rules of the game' for entering foreign markets, and building that experience takes time. Thus, whilst firms such as HNA, Dalian Wanda, Anbang, and Fosun have spent over $100 billion on a wide range of assets apparently unconnected to firm-specific advantage (FSA) or country-specific advantage (CSA), these moves lack apparent industrial logic. Concerns over risks are raised by experts and policymakers. These concerns are deepened by evidence of unsound financing structures with high levels of debt, all adding to a sense of high risk, with potential implications beyond Chinese firms.

A more positive view is the argument that a holistic and long-term perspective should be taken to Chinese firms internationalising their operations. Losses and failures are normal at an early stage of internationalising strategy, and the experience gained is invaluable for the future. An important way of knowing a foreign market is to acquire practical experience in the way that Hauwei, Xiaomi, and Haier are doing. These firms, and others, may see international expansion as a dynamic learning and feedback process. Thus, early mistakes may provide experience for the future, in a 'learning-by-investing' approach. However, as these firms embark on a new international crusade, it is important to remember that nations like Britain — with examples such as the East India Company, which dates to 1600 — have a long history of cross-border investments and developing world-class executives. International firms from many Western nations tend to have a deeply imbedded 'administrative heritage' in international markets, which creates a significant competitive advantage.

Given the strategic disadvantages, a legitimate question is why do Chinese firms go overseas when there may be a high opportunity costs to doing business in their own domestic market, where none of the liability of foreignness costs exist and social networks are stronger? The evidence suggests that several factors explain the internationalisation of Chinese firms. The first is the acquisition of advanced technology and R&D capabilities, as is evident in Huawei and Haier. The second is the acquisition of resources that are in short supply in the domestic market. The third is the acquisition of global brands that would otherwise take too long to create, if that were possible. An additional reason can be broadly categorised as the institutional factor that encourage Chinese firms to expand internationally for institutionally 'embedded' reasons rather than reflecting a strategic firm choice. Thus, consistent with the Fifth C hypothesis, incentives from government in the form of generous bank loans (low interest rates and high leverage) and soft budget constraints (acceptance of financial outcomes that an economically rational investor would not accept) are some of the incentives that lead firms to follow an international path at the request or with the encouragement of government.

Within the Four C's framework, Chinese firms are not yet endowed with the depth of management competence needed to confidently state that the DNA of Chinese management is equipped for international markets. Nor, because of the biases that exist towards China such as negative media and other forms of discrimination, are Chinese firms advantaged by their country of origin; indeed, the opposite is true. Nor is cultural adaptability an asset, with Western societies finding Chinese culture and language as impenetrable as the Great Wall of China. The absence of any clear FSA or a shared CSA as a basis for expanding internationally suggests that the weakness of Chinese firms in one or more of the Cs is compensated

Table 1:   Four C's Comparison Across Countries

Four Cs	China	US	UK	Australia	Japan
Core capabilities	2	5	4	4	4
Cultural adaptability	1	4	5	4	2
Competencies of management	1	5	4	4	4
Country of origin	2	5	5	5	4
Four C's total	**6**	**19**	**18**	**17**	**14**
Cooperation of government	5	2	2	2	3
Overall total	**11**	**21**	**20**	**19**	**17**

by a Fifth C in the form of cooperation with government. The evidence to support this hypothesis is compelling and allows an understanding of strategic moves that existing theory would otherwise describe as a puzzle, raising red flags as to the likelihood of the significant investment producing any economic value.

Table 1 evaluates the Four Cs across selected countries to highlight relevant comparison and areas of weakness for Chinese firms. This is a largely anecdotal approach, building in part on the findings from Bloom *et al.* (2012) and much of the evidence from the research cited throughout this book. In the simple framework taken to the assessment: 1 — very weak; 2 — weak; 3 — satisfactory; 4 — strong; and 5 — very strong.

The weaknesses of Chinese firms in many of the Four Cs attributes for success in international markets do not lead to a questioning of the undoubted ability (as evidenced by Alibaba, Tencent, Xiaomi, and many others) of Chinese management to create new and highly innovative domestic businesses. The entrepreneurial spirit in China stands up to comparison with any other nation. Indeed, the rise of the POEs, despite the many barriers, is testimony to the drive of the Chinese people. Significantly, in many industries, there is now ample evidence of Chinese innovation outpacing the Western equivalent. Though Haft (2015) claims, 'I do not know of a single company that tries to imitate Chinese business practice', time will no doubt provide many examples. Complacency on the part of Western businesses could expose them to the risks the US automotive industry faced when it dismissed the innovation, quality control, lean production, and productivity of their Japanese competitors in the 1970s, as described in Womack *et al.* (1990) in the excellent book *The Machines That Changed the World*. The advanced manufacturing techniques at Toyota, then half the size of General Motors, eventually saw Toyota overtake GM as the world's largest car manufacturer. Who would bet against Chinese firms eventually achieving similar success against complacent Western 'champions'? Management consulting firm McKinsey & Co. predict that, by 2025, close to 45% of the *Fortune 500* will be based in emerging economies, and China will no doubt have a disproportionate share. Will these firms have a high TNI, though, as discussed in Chapter 1? Will they be truly global firms? Can they become 'system integrators', as described by Professor Nolan?

Consistent with the hypothesis of weak management capabilities and soft budget constraints, Tse (2015: 136) notes the poor performance of investments made by Chinese firms to date: 'due to a combination of inexperience and a lack of accountability, many state-owned companies heavily overpaid for their purchases and then had trouble digesting them'. This is a concern. Firms that fail to achieve return on invested capital (ROIC) at least equal to their risk-adjusted cost of capital operate at a loss in an economic sense regardless of their reported accounting-based profits, such firms return less to the economy than they consume in resources, thus destroying wealth. If this process is widespread and prolonged, macro-economic consequences may ensue, these can take years to manifest, but manifest they will. To ignore this reality is to add to the potential risks already evident in the Chinese economy and create the conditions for a re-run of the experience of many internationally minded Japanese firms in the 1980s, which, with access to cheap money from accommodating banks, overpaid for assets that they ultimately were unable to integrate and manage. In paying for their 'irrational exuberance' Japanese firms and the economy has experienced what amounts to at least a 'lost decade' of development and growth.

The truism that financial capability does not equate to management capability in international markets is a sober reality. Chinese firms do not have the 'administrative heritage' that allows ease of entry to new markets, which can be viewed as a form of first-mover advantage enjoyed largely by Western firms. This can be thought of in terms of 'hardware' and 'software'. The *hardware* of the firm is the physical assets, including capital and structures, that are visible internally and externally and can be replicated by others. A firm's *software* is the unique heritage — its human capital and culture — that has been developed over many years and is deeply rooted in its DNA. SOEs, often operating in protected structures in their domestic market, are on the surface poor candidates for internationalisation because they are unlikely to have developed the management competencies needed to operate in competitive markets. Conversely, firms like Huawei and Haier, who are exposed to strong domestic competition and ostensibly little government protection, are better placed to compete in overseas markets. Their focus on localising their international networks (e.g. R&D centres) is an evidence of growing maturity in Chinese firms and an ability to build global businesses.

Given the dominance of Western influence in business, there is a temptation to assume that, as Chinese managers mature in the international economy, a gradual convergence with Western practices will occur and that management theory and practice will fall into line. It is too early to formulate an informed opinion on this, except to note the advice from Hofstede (1984):

> Convergence of management will never come. What we can bring about is an understanding of how culture affects our thinking differently from other people's thinking and what this means for the transfer of management practices and theories.

National culture will influence international practices, and the existence of biases cannot be ignored. Culture will always influence how a firm responds to its environment, but the predictive power of cultural analysis is limited. Management philosophies are thus bound to differ, given the strong cultural differences that exist, as is evident in the Confucian and agrarian influences on Chinese executives, combined with the influence of contemporary politics.

As China becomes a knowledge-driven economy, consistent with President Xi's goals of 'transitioning to innovation-driven growth', completing the building of a moderately prosperous society in all respects by 2021, and achieving the aspirations of 'Made in China 2025', a natural conclusion is that the quality of leadership and management will be pivotal and that management education will be critical to the success of Chinese firms in the international economy. However, this is not to argue that management education is enough to underpin success. The evidence from Bloom *et al.* (2012), discussed in Chapters 7 and 8, is compelling. Globally, there is a sense of a crisis of identity and a questioning of the relevance of management education after decades of strong growth. In part, this might be linked to the crisis identity facing capitalism and democracy. As is evident in the primary research, the demand for management education is unlikely to decline, but the 'product' must meet the market. As the *Financial Times* noted,[5] 'The future of management education is bright — provided business schools broaden the scope of who they serve and how they serve them'. The main criticism is that most business schools approach the market with a supply-side mentality: Who can take the programmes we want to offer at the price we want to charge? Instead, a demand-side philosophy would ask: Who needs management education, and how can we provide it to them?' This paradigm shift will be critical to management education's ability to realise its potential in contributing to the success of Chinese firms. The research provides strong signals that businesses want management education but want it to be more relevant to their needs. The view that such education should have 'Chinese characteristics' is not strongly supported but shouldn't be discounted. There is much to the philosophy that business and economic principles, like those of medicine, transcend geographies and markets; the importance of cross-cultural management should never be understated, however, though it is all too easy to do so.

Given how underweight Chinese firms are in the global economy, it is a fair assumption that overseas direct investment will be an ongoing feature of the global economy in the years ahead, even

---

[5] *Financial Times*, April 27, 2015, 'Business schools are their own worst enemies'.

excluding the exciting OBOR strategy. The theoretical evidence points to the reality that the nature of their competitive advantage is often unclear, and the strategic and industrial logic can sometimes look like *crossing the river by feeling the stones.* It is no surprise, then, that the performance of the clear majority of Chinese firms that have gone global is not encouraging and that the high level of financial leverage appears both unsustainable and concerning, whilst the opaque nature of corporate governance remains a concern. A positive view is that the Chinese firms leading the way in international markets are early pioneers, and lessons will be learnt that will benefit future generations. This is a generous interpretation given the deep-rooted cultural challenges and biases at play. Even the most able managers in the world from nations and firms steeped in the Four Cs would be hard-pressed to navigate the biases and insurmountable challenges Chinese firms are facing. There is no avoiding the reality that, if Chinese firms are to succeed, their success will be largely determined by the quality of the management charged with their stewardship. The Bloom *et al.*'s (2012) comparisons of relative management competencies, discussed in Chapter 7, underline the scale of the task Chinese management face, before adding the five biases, which in aggregate only underscore the insurmountable challenges that Chinese firms in global markets face. All the challenges and constraints, both hard and soft, place a premium on the quality of management if any firm is to succeed internationally, as *businesses do not fail; it's management that fails.*

Appendix 1

Research Methodology

As with any research, the findings are greatly influenced by the methodology. Thus, a background description of the methodology is useful to a reader interested in such detail.

The primary research used in this book employed a multidisciplinary methodology, following Hucznyski's (1996) advice on how to construct a successful management research idea: (i) it must address a topical problem (*the what*), (ii) it must relate to the needs and concerns of management and other stakeholders (*the why*), and (iii) it should be presented in an effective and engaging manner (*the how*).

A positivism paradigm was adopted as the core of the research strategy. Positivism is based on the ontological principle that the truth is independent of the researcher. This allows for quantifiable observations and a hypothesis- and deduction-based research using statistical analysis. Consistent with this approach, the researcher concentrates on the facts and remains independent. As Dudovskiy (2015: 10) notes, 'if you assume a positivist approach to your study, then it is your belief that you are independent of your research and your research can be purely objective'. Positivism as an epistemology is subject to several weaknesses. For example, the research findings may only be descriptive and can lack deep insights. The research strategy also adopted a triangulation approach by using multiple sources of data and both qualitative and quantitative methods. It is not uncommon to use triangulation in business research, as it allows for a broader, complementary view of the research question.

However, such an approach must form part of the design at the outset rather than a default position from a poorly designed methodology. Consistent with a triangulation approach, an extensive literature review was conducted, and the primary data were complemented by secondary data.

The core of the research approach was survey-based fieldwork and a review of secondary data from a 2014 KPMG/University of Sydney email survey questionnaire of Chinese firms in Australia, which resulted in 51 responses (20 SOEs and 31 POEs). The sample consisted of Chinese firms actively invested outside China and those planning to do so. The dataset included firms from multiple industries. The target sample size of 88 firms resulted in responses from 54 firms (a 61% response rate), which is considered statistically significant. Of the 54 firms, 20 were SOEs and 34 POEs. The interviewees were senior executives who had influence on human resource management and international strategy. Demographic details on the survey respondents can be found in Appendix 4.

Data Collection & Interpretation

The involvement of three professionally connected, Chinese-born, and Mandarin-speaking individuals known to the researcher allowed the researcher to leverage the strength of existing relationships, enhancing the quality of the information/knowledge obtained. As Andrew and Delahaye (2000) observed, people are more willing to share information with others if they trust them, which is particularly relevant to executives at Chinese firms. The involvement of the three 'research assistants' also helped address cultural factors, as highlighted by Hofstede (1993) in his five-dimensional model of national cultural difference, in which power distance can influence data integrity. Data collection occurred in three stages, all standardised through a questionnaire-based survey instrument (see Appendix 2) free from interviewer bias: (i) personal interviews were conducted using existing networks of relations, although the survey instrument was emailed to some respondents, if requested by them, (ii) interviews took place across 54 firms, and (iii) data/interviews were conducted during June and July 2015, with 85% of the respondents Australia-based, consistent with the sampling frame of the KPMG/University of Sydney survey.

The bias towards Chinese firms in Australia should not weaken the relevance of the research on Chinese firms in a global sense. Until 2012, Australia was the largest recipient of Chinese investment, and whilst there was initially a weighting towards natural resources, this has changed in recent years. The KPMG/University of Sydney research highlights the role that Australia plays as a first-mover stepping stone in the internationalisation process of Chinese firms. This in part reflects the fact that Australia, a mature and highly regulated developed economy, still retains comparative advantages relative to other countries, including geography, as a home for Chinese OFDI. Moreover, 65% of the firms surveyed operate in two or more countries outside China, with 41% operating in three or more countries. The data covered only investments in which the Chinese firm owned or had legal control over the operating business.

The survey instrument contained a provision for quantitative data capture and qualitative interview-style comments. The data collection and the questions were highly specific and precise and were largely conducted as structured interviews. The researcher was mindful of the advice of Farh *et al.* (2006) on the importance of ensuring a contextually valid survey instrument relevant to a Chinese context in order to avoid flawed findings and perceived knowledge: 'Given the large cultural distance between China and the West, simple translation of Western measures may not yield adequate instruments for Chinese contexts' (Farh *et al.*, 2006: 307). This risk is prevalent in management research given the dominance of Western approaches and, as Farh *et al.* (2006: 305) point out, the 'paucity of locally developed measures in China' for a Chinese context. Translation risk from Mandarin to English was mitigated through the involvement of three Mandarin-speaking assistants. English was used in all but five of the 54 completed surveys. The involvement of Mandarin-speaking research assistants also ensured that the contextualisation advice of Tsui (2006: 9) was applied in gathering the data: 'To further Chinese management research and develop valid knowledge, contextualisation in measurement is not only desirable, but essential'. The research design ensured that the four tests of a valid measurement instrument were met: (i) validity, (ii) stability, (iii) internal reliability, and (iv) inter-observer consistency. The focus of the survey was on assessing the importance that firms place on having internationally experienced management; the extent to which this is currently an issue; the nature of the issues (e.g. constraints on strategic intent); the importance of management education in addressing the issues; satisfaction with available forms of management education; the extent to which 'Western' models of management education are appropriate; the significance of cultural education.

Each of the statements in the survey was framed on a seven-point Likert scale, where the respondents were asked to select answers from the scale. The quantitative and qualitative scales were 7 for *Very Strongly Agree*, 6 for *Strongly Agree*, 5 for *Agree*, 4 for *Not/Neutral*, 3 for *Disagree*, 2 for *Strongly Disagree*, and 1 for *Very Strongly Disagree*. The goal was to obtain data and insights that have universal validity for Chinese firms in the international economy, whilst acknowledging the bias towards Chinese firms in Australia for data collection purposes.

Summary of the Responses to Questions 1–8

Question	Mean	SD
International expansion is important to our firm's success	2.2	1.2
Internationally experienced staff are important for our success in foreign markets	1.9	0.8
Insufficient internationally experienced senior management is a constraint on our firm's growth strategy	2.5	1.3
Senior management in each country must have experience in the local market	2.1	1.2
Senior management outside China must understand the Chinese market	2.3	1.3
Senior management in foreign subs. should have experience in working in China at HO	2.7	1.2
Non-Chinese senior management should understand Chinese culture	2.2	1.0
Non-Chinese senior management should speak Mandarin	3.6	1.3

Summary of the Responses to Questions 9–18

Question	Mean	SD
Management Education is important to our international strategy	2.2	0.8
Management Education is important in building management capabilities needed to succeed overseas	2.4	0.9
Cross-cultural management is important to our firm's international strategy	2.1	0.8
MBA qualified executives will be preferred in international appointments	3.3	1.2
Management Education with 'Chinese characteristics' is important to the development of management talent	3.1	1.2
In hiring young executives, formal Management Education is preferred	2.9	1.1
Management training within the business is preferred to external programs	3.1	1.0
Difficult to assess the value of the investment in Management Education	3.9	1.1
Management Education is too theoretical and not relevant to business needs	4.2	1.1
Highly educated executives are difficult to retain	3.7	1.1

Appendix 2

Primary Research Questionnaire

Academic Research Survey into the Importance of Management Education to Chinese Firms in the International Economy

June–July 2015

The Survey

First, some general information about yourself which is helpful in aggregate analysis

Your age

☐ Under 30   ☐ 45–54   ☐ I prefer not to respond
☐ 30–44   ☐ 55 or over

Your gender

☐ Female   ☐ Male   ☐ I prefer not to respond

Your education level

☐ High School   ☐ Master Degree
☐ I prefer not to respond ☐ Bachelor Degree
☐ PhD

Firm's annual turnover (A$m)?

☐ Less than 50 million   ☐ Between 100–200 million
☐ More than 500 million   ☐ Less than 100 million
☐ Between 200–500 million

Number of countries the firm operates in?

☐ One   ☐ Three   ☐ Five or more
☐ Two   ☐ Four

1. International expansion is important to our firm's future success

☐ Very Strongly Agree   ☐ Agree   ☐ Disagree
☐ Strongly Agree   ☐ Neutral ☑ Strongly Disagree
☐ Very Strongly Disagree

2. Internationally experienced staff are important for our success in foreign markets

☐ Very Strongly Agree   ☐ Agree   ☐ Disagree
☐ Strongly Agree   ☐ Neutral ☐ Strongly Disagree
☐ Very Strongly Disagree

3. Insufficient internationally experienced senior management is a constraint on our firm's growth strategy

☐ Very Strongly Agree   ☐ Agree   ☐ Disagree
☐ Strongly Agree   ☐ Neutral ☐ Strongly Disagree
☐ Very Strongly Disagree

4. Senior management in each country must have experience in the local market

---

☐ Very Strongly Agree   ☐ Agree   ☐ Disagree
☐ Strongly Agree   ☐ Neutral   ☐ Strongly Disagree
☐ Very Strongly Disagree

5. Senior management in each country outside China must understand the Chinese market

---

☐ Very Strongly Agree   ☐ Agree   ☐ Disagree
☐ Strongly Agree   ☐ Neutral   ☐ Strongly Disagree
☐ Very Strongly Disagree

6. Senior management in foreign subsidiaries should have work experience in China at the parent company

---

☐ Very Strongly Agree   ☐ Agree   ☐ Disagree
☐ Strongly Agree   ☐ Neutral   ☐ Strongly Disagree
☐ Very Strongly Disagree

7. Non-Chinese senior management in each country should understand Chinese culture

---

☐ Very Strongly Agree   ☐ Agree   ☐ Disagree
☐ Strongly Agree   ☐ Neutral   ☐ Strongly Disagree
☐ Very Strongly Disagree

8. Non-Chinese senior management in each country should speak Mandarin

---

☐ Very Strongly Agree   ☐ Agree   ☐ Disagree
☐ Strongly Agree   ☐ Neutral   ☐ Strongly Disagree
☐ Very Strongly Disagree

9. Management education is important in the future to our international strategy

---

☐ Very Strongly Agree ☐ Agree ☐ Disagree
☐   Strongly Agree ☐ Neutral ☐ Strongly Disagree
☐ Very Strongly Disagree

10. Management education is important in building management capabilities needed to succeed in foreign markets

---

☐ Very Strongly Agree ☐ Agree ☐ Disagree
☐   Strongly Agree ☐ Neutral ☐ Strongly Disagree
☐ Very Strongly Disagree

11. Cross-cultural awareness is important to our firm's international strategy

---

☐ Very Strongly Agree ☐ Agree ☐ Disagree
☐   Strongly Agree ☐ Neutral ☐ Strongly Disagree
☐ Very Strongly Disagree

12. MBA qualified (or equivalent) executives will increasingly be preferred in senior international appointments in foreign markets

---

☐ Very Strongly Agree ☐ Agree ☐ Disagree
☐   Strongly Agree ☐ Neutral ☐ Strongly Disagree
☐ Very Strongly Disagree

13. Management education with 'Chinese characteristics' rather than 'Western' programs will be important in the future development of management talent for Chinese firms

---

☐ Very Strongly Agree ☐ Agree ☐ Disagree
☐   Strongly Agree ☐ Neutral ☐ Strongly Disagree
☐ Very Strongly Disagree

14. In hiring young executives (i.e. under 30 years), formal management education is preferred

☐ Very Strongly Agree ☐ Agree ☐ Disagree
☐ Strongly Agree ☐ Neutral ☐ Strongly Disagree
☐ Very Strongly Disagree

15. Management training within the business is preferred to external programs

☐ Very Strongly Agree ☐ Agree ☐ Disagree
☐ Strongly Agree ☐ Neutral ☐ Strongly Disagree
☐ Very Strongly Disagree

16. It is difficult to assess the value of the investment made in management education

☐ Very Strongly Agree ☐ Agree ☐ Disagree
☐ Strongly Agree ☐ Neutral ☐ Strongly Disagree
☐ Very Strongly Disagree

17. Management education is too theoretical and not relevant to business needs

☐ Very Strongly Agree ☐ Agree ☐ Disagree
☐ Strongly Agree ☐ Neutral ☐ Strongly Disagree
☐ Very Strongly Disagree

18. Highly educated executives are difficult to retain

☐ Very Strongly Agree ☐ Agree ☐ Disagree
☐ Strongly Agree ☐ Neutral ☐ Strongly Disagree
☐ Very Strongly Disagree

General Questions

1. Are there any general comments you would make on the importance or relevance of management education?
2. What industry or field is your business in?

Thank you very much for taking the time to complete this survey. Your input is valued and very much appreciated!

Appendix 3

KPMG/University of Sydney Survey of Chinese Firms Invested in Australia (Extracts: Full Survey Details Can Be Found at www.kpmg.com.au)

1. When you make investment decisions in Australia, how important are the following points? Scale from 0 to 10

1. Making a profit	8.25
2. Securing resources	7.39
3. Access to global markets	6.52
4. Acquiring new technologies	5.17
5. Introducing own technology to international market	5.68
6. Building up international brand name	6.53
7. Availability of finance	5.25
8. Stock market listing	4.94
9. Gaining experience for operating in other markets	6.19
10. Links with other Chinese investors	6.54
11. Export to Australian market	5.46
12. Acquiring management know-how	6.50

2. **Australian business leaders are supportive towards Chinese investment**

Strongly Disagree	0%
Disagree	6%
Neutral	35%
Agree	55%
Strongly Agree	4%
Total Responses	100%

3. **Chinese investors feel welcome to invest in Australia**

Strongly Disagree	2%
Disagree	15%
Neutral	31%
Agree	48%
Strongly Agree	4%
Total Responses	100%

4. **Australian media are supportive towards Chinese**

Strongly Disagree	8%
Disagree	34%
Neutral	42%
Agree	16%
Strongly Agree	0%
Total Responses	100%

5. **Australia is more welcoming to investors from other countries than to Chinese investors**

Strongly Disagree	0%
Disagree	22%
Neutral	28%
Agree	37%
Strongly Agree	13%
Total Responses	100%

6. **Chinese executives find it easy to work with Australian executives**

Strongly Disagree	4%
Disagree	24%
Neutral	34%
Agree	32%
Strongly Agree	6%
Total Responses	100%

7. **Chinese investors find it difficult to work with trade unions**

Strongly Disagree	0%
Disagree	2%
Neutral	45%
Agree	39%
Strongly Agree	14%
Total Responses	100%

8. **Chinese and Australian board members find it difficult to understand each other**

Strongly Disagree	0%
Disagree	14%
Neutral	54%
Agree	28%
Strongly Agree	4%
Total Responses	100%

9. **Takeovers are easier to manage than joint ventures**

Strongly Disagree	2%
Disagree	12%
Neutral	31%
Agree	45%
Strongly Agree	10%
Total Responses	100%

10. **Chinese investors prefer having majority control**

Strongly Disagree	2%
Disagree	8%
Neutral	312%
Agree	58%
Strongly Agree	20%
Total Responses	100%

11. **My head office colleagues feel they need more information about Australia**

Strongly Disagree	0%
Disagree	0%
Neutral	10%
Agree	65%
Strongly Agree	24%
Total Responses	100%

Appendix 4

Survey of 54 Chinese Firms on Their International Strategy

Demographics

Age		Gender		Education	
<30	9	Male	34 (63%)	High School	1
30–44	22	Female	20 (37%)	Bachelor	25
45–54	16			Masters	24
55>	7			PhD	4

Turnover

<$50 million	19	35%
<$100 million	9	17%
<$200 million	1	
<$500 million	3	6%
>$500 million	22	41%

Number of Countries Operating outside China

One	19	35%
Two	13	24%
Three	4	7%
Four	3	6%
Five or more	15	28%

Appendix 5

Chronology of the 'Century of Humiliation'

1839–1860	Period of the Opium Wars and unequal treaties (1842 Treaty of Nanking ending Opium Wars; 1860 occupation of Peking by British and French forces)
1850–1881	Period of revolts and rebellions (1850–1864 Taiping Rebellion; 1853–1868 Nian Rebellion, also Shanghai, Moslem, and Miao revolts)
1894–1895	China defeated by Japan
1897–1898	Scramble for concessions by Germany, Britain, Russia, and France
1898	Hundred Days' reform
1900	Boxer uprising
1901–1911	The decade of conservative reform: abolition of examination system (1905); programme to send thousands of students abroad to study; preparation for constitutional monarchy
1904–1905	Russo-Japanese War, fought on Chinese territory
1905	Sun Yat-sen organises Revolutionary League amongst Chinese students in Tokyo
1911–1912	Republican revolution, abdication of the Manchus and the establishment of the Republic of China

1915	Japan presents Twenty-One Demands. 'New Culture Movement' founded to promote values of science and democracy
1916–1926	Warlord period. Failure of republicanism
1919	May Fourth Movement. Treaty of Versailles
1921	Founding of the Chinese Communist Party
1923–1927	Nationalist–communist United Front
1925	May 30th Anti-foreigner Movement
1927	Chiang Kia-shek crushes communists in Shanghai and Nanking. Beginning of 10-year phase of Nationalist government
1937	War with Japan begins
1945	End of war with Japan
1946	Beginning of Civil War
1949	Establishment of People's Republic of China

Appendix 6

Chronology of Major Economic and Social Events in China Since 1911

1911	Republican Revolution
1914–1918	World War I
1917	Russian Revolution
1919	Versailles Treaty, not signed by China
1919	May Fourth Movement sweeps the main cities
1919	Deng Xiaoping and Zhou Enlai study in France
1921	Birth of the CCP
1927	Start of the Chinese Civil War
1931	Japanese invasion of Manchuria
1934	Start of the Long March
1937	Sino-Japanese War
1939–1945	World War II
1941–1948	Hyperinflation
1941	Attack on Pearl Harbour
1945	Japanese surrender
1949	Mao Zedong takes power and proclaims the PRC
1949	Nationalists retreat to Taiwan
1949–1952	Land reforms and collectivization
1950–1953	Early industrialisation and nationalisation
1950–1953	Korean War
1953	First Five-Year Plan
1954–1956	Agriculture collectivisation

1956	Industry socialised
1956	'Let a Hundred Flowers Bloom'
1957	Anti-Rightist campaign
1958–1960	Great Leap Forward
1958	Launch of the communes
1960	Sino-Soviet split
1966	Beginning of the Cultural Revolution
1972	President Nixon visits China
1975	Four modernisations announced
1976	Death of Mao Zedong and Zhou Enlai
1976	Hua Guofeng succeeds Mao
1978–1992	Deng Xiaoping as paramount leader
1978	Deng Xiaoping launches economic reforms
1979	Diplomatic relations with the US resumed
1979	One-child policy proclaimed
1980	Special economic zones set-up
1985	Urban private enterprise permitted
1989	Tiananmen Square demonstrations
1989	Jiang Zemin becomes party secretary
1992	Russia and China sign declaration restoring ties
1997	Death of Deng Xiaoping at age 92
1997	Handover of Hong Kong
1998	Zhu Rongi succeeds Li Peng as premier
2001	Entry to WTO
2002	Hu Jintao becomes president, Wen Jiabao, premier
2003	SARS epidemic
2002	Over 200 million Internet users in China
2005	President Hu Jintao launches the 'Harmonious Society' social movement
2007	A new Roman Catholic Bishop of Beijing is consecrated
2008	Sichuan earthquake kills tens of thousands
2008	Beijing Olympics
2009	Sixty-year anniversary of the PRC
2011	China overtakes Japan as the second-largest economy

2012	Official figures suggest city dwellers outnumber rural population
2013	Xi Jinping becomes president
2015	One-child policy ended
2016	Economic growth at 6.9% in 2015 is lowest level for 25 years
2017	President Xi confirmed as China's paramount leader drawing comparisons to Chairman Mao

Source: Warner 2014, adapted from miscellaneous sources.

Bibliography

Abrams, Regina, Kirby, William, and McFarlan, Warren, 2014a, *Can China Lead? Reaching the Limits of Power and Growth,* Boston: Harvard Business Review Press.

Abrami, Regina, Kirby, William, and McFarlan, Warren, 2014b, *Why China Can't Innovate,* Boston: Harvard Business Review.

Aden, Christopher H. and Bartels, Larry M., 2016, *Democracy for Realists: Why Elections Do Not Produce Responsive Governments,* Princeton, N.J.: Princeton University Press.

Allison, Graham, 2017, *Destined for War: Can America and China Escape Thucydides's Trap?* New York: Houghton Mifflin Harcourt.

Alon, Ilan *et al.,* 2013, Internationalisation of Chinese entrepreneurial firms, *Thunderbird International Business Review,* 55(5), 469–483.

Alon, Ilan and Lu, Le, 2004, The state of marketing and business education in China, *Marketing Education Review,* 14(1).

Alon, Ilan, 2003, *Chinese Culture, Organisational Behaviour and International Business Management,* Westport: Praeger.

Alon, Ilan and McIntyre, John R. (eds.), 2005, *Business and Management Education in China: Transition, Pedagogy and Training,* Singapore: World Scientific Pub Co.

Alon, Ilan and McIntyre, John R. (eds.), 2008, *Globalisation of Chinese Enterprises,* New York: Palgrave Macmillan.

Alon, Ilan and Chang, Julian (eds.), 2009, *China Rules: Globalisation and Political Transformation,* New York: Palgrave Macmillan.

Alon, Ilan and Jones, Victoria (eds.), 2013, *Innovation in Business Education in Emerging Markets,* New York: Palgrave Macmillan.

Alon, Ilan, Yeheskel, Orly, Lerner, Miri, and Zhang, Wenxian, 2013, Internationalization of Chinese entrepreneurial firms, *Thunderbird International Business Review,* 55(5), 495.

Andrew, Kate M. and Delahaye, Brian L., 2000, Influence of knowledge processes in organisational learning: The psychosocial filter, *Journal of Management Studies*, 37(6), 797–810.

Armstrong, Steven and Fukami, Cynthia, V. (eds.), 2009, *The SAGE Handbook of Management Learning, Education and Development*, Thousand Oaks: SAGE Publication.

Bai, Xue and Enderwick, Peter, 2005, *Economic Transition and Management Skills: The Case of China*, in Alon, Ilan and McIntyre, John R. (eds.), *Business and Management Education in China: Transition, Pedagogy and Training*, Singapore: World Scientific Pub Co., pp. 21–45.

Barker, Richard, 2010, *The Big Idea: No, Management Is Not a Profession*, Boston: Harvard Business Review, July–August.

Bartlett, Christopher A. and Ghoshal, Sumantra, 2002, *Managing Across Borders: The Transnational Solution*, 2nd edn., Boston: Harvard Business Review Press.

Barney, Jay, 1991, Firm resources and sustained competitive advantage, *Journal of Management*, 17(1), 99–120.

Barney, Jay, Wright, Mike, and Ketchen, David, 2001, The Resource-based view of the firm: Ten years after 1991, *Journal of Management*, 27, 625–641.

Beamish, Paul W. and Bapuji, Hari, 2008, Toy recalls and China: Emotion vs. evidence, *Management and Organisation Review*, 4(2), 197–210.

Beardson, Timothy, 2013, *Stumbling Giant — The Threats to China's Future*, New Haven: Yale University Press.

Bell, Daniel A., 2015, *The China Model — Political Meritocracy and the Limits of Democracy*, Princeton and Oxford: Princeton University Press.

Berrell, Mike, Wrathall, Jeff, and Wright, Phil, 2001, A model for Chinese management education: Adapting the case study method to transfer management knowledge, *Cross Cultural Management*, 8(1), 28–43.

Bickers, Robert, 2017, *Out of China — How the Chinese Ended the Era of Western Domination*, London: Allen Lane, Penguin Random House.

Birkinshaw, Julian and Piramal, Gita (eds.) 2005, *Sumantra Ghoshal on Management*, Upper Saddle River: FT Prentice-Hall.

Birnbaum, Robert, 2000, *Management Fads in Higher Education: Where They Come From, What They Do, Why They Fail*, New York: Jossey-Bass.

Bloom, Nicholas and Van Reenen, John, 2007, Measuring and explaining management practices firms and countries, *Quarterly Journal of Economics*, 122(4), 1341–1408.

Bloom, Nicholas, Genakos, Christos, Sadun, Raffaella, and Van Reenen, John, 2012, *Management Practices Across Firms and Countries*, National

Bureau of Economic Research, Working Paper 17850, http://www.nber.org/papers/w17850.

Boisot, Max and Meyer, Marshall W., 2008, Which way through the open door? Reflections on the internationalization of Chinese firms. *Management and Organization Review*, 4(3), 349–365.

Booz & Co., 2007, *The Next Management Crisis in China: Developing and Retaining Highly Skilled Young Managers*, New York: Booz & Co.

Briscoe, Dennis, Schuler, Randall, and Tarique, Ibraiz, 2004, *International Human Resource Management*, London: Routledge.

Brown, Archie, 2011, The *Rise and Fall of Communism*, Manhattan: Ecco Press.

Brown, Gordon, 2010, *Beyond the Crash*, London: Simon & Schuster.

Brown, Kerry, 2014, *The New Emperors — Power and the Princelings in China*, London: I.B. Tauris & Co.

Brown, Kerry, 2015, *The Maoists and Modern China*, Policy Paper No. 9, China Studies Centre, University of Sydney. http://sydney.edu.au/china studies centre.

Bryant, Nick, *The Rise and Fall of Australia — How a Great Nation Lost its Way*, Bantam, 2015, p. 238.

Bryman, Alan, 2006, Social *Research Methods*, 3rd edn., Oxford: Oxford University Press.

Buckley, Peter J., Clegg, Jeremy, L., Cross, Adam R., Xin, Liu, Voss, Hinrich, and Ping, Zheng, 2007, The determinants of Chinese outward foreign direct investment, *Journal of International Business Studies*, 34(4), 499–518.

Callahan, William, A., 2010, *China — The Pessoptimist Nation*, Oxford: Oxford University Press.

Cardenal, Juan Pablo and Araujo, Herberto, 2013, *China's Silent Army: The Pioneers, Traders, Fixers and Workers Who Are Remaking the World in Beijing's Image*, New York: Crown.

Cen, Zilan, 2013, *Chinese OFDI in Australia: Drivers and Entry Mode*, PhD dissertation, University of Tasmania.

Chen, Ming-Jer, 2001, *Inside Chinese Business*, Boston: Harvard Business School Press.

Chen, Haiyang, Griffith, David A., and Hu, Michael Y., 2006, The Influence of liability of foreignness on market entry strategies: An illustration of market entry in China, *International Marketing Review*, 23(6), 636–649.

Child, John, 1972, Organisational structure, environment and performance, *Sociology*, 6, 1–22.

Child, John and Mollering, Guido, 2003, Contextual confidence and active trust development in the Chinese business environment, *Organisation Science*, 14(1), 69–80.

Child, John and Rodrigues, Suzana. B., 2005, The internationalisation of Chinese firms: A case for theoretical extension? *Management and Organisation Review*, 1(3), 381–410.

Cohen, Raymond, 2001, Resolving conflict across languages, *Negotiation Journal*, 17(1), 17–34.

Collins, James C. and Porras, Jeremy I., 1994, *Built to Last: Successful Habits of Visionary Companies*, New York City, HarperBusiness.

Collis, Jill and Hussey, Roger, 2009, *Business Research*, 3rd edn., in London: Palgrave Macmillan.

Cooke, Fang Lee, 2008, *Competition Strategy and Management in China*, London: Palgrave Macmillan.

Cooke, Fang Lee, 2009, A decade of transformation of HRM in China: A review of literature and suggestions of future studies, *Asia Pacific Journal of Human Resources*, 47(1), 6–40.

Dahlam, Carl and Zeng, Zhihua Douglad, 2007, *Enhancing China's Competitiveness through Lifelong Learning* (WBI Development Studies), Washington: World Bank Publication.

Datar, Srikant, Garvin, David A., and Cullen, Patrick G., 2010, *Rethinking the MBA: Business Education at a Crossroads*, Boston: Harvard Business Review Press.

Datta, Deepak K. and Puia, George, 1995, Cross-border acquisitions: An examination of the influence of relatedness and cultural fit on shareholder value creation in U.S. acquiring firms, *Management International Review*, 35(4), 337–359.

De Grauwe, Paul, 2017, *The Limits of the Market: The Pendulum between Government and Market*, Oxford: Oxford University Press.

Deng, Shengliang and Wang, Yinglou, 1992, Management education in China: Past, present and future, *World Development*, 20(6), 873–880.

Deng, Ping, 2007, Investing for strategic resources and its rationale: The case of outward FDI from Chinese companies, *Business Horizons*, 50(1), 71–81.

Deng, Ping, 2009, Why Do Chinese firms tend to acquire strategic assets in international expansion? *Journal of World Business*, 44(1), 74–84.

Deng Xiaoping, 1993, *Building a Socialism with a Specifically Chinese Character*, Selected Works, Vol. 3, Beijing: People's Publishing House.

Dickson, Bruce J., 2008, *Wealth into Power: The Communist CCP's Embrace of the Private Sector*, Cambridge, UK: Cambridge University Press.

Doz, Yves L. and Prahalad, Coimbatore K., 1994, Managing DMNCs: A search for a new paradigm, in Rumelt, Richard P., Schendel, Dan E., and Teece, David J. (eds.), *Fundamental Issues in Strategy*, Boston: Harvard Business School Press, pp. 495–526.

Eden, Lorraine and Miller, Stewart R., 2004, Distance matters: Liability of foreignness, institutional distance, and ownership strategy, *Advances in International Management*, 16, 187–221.

Elger, Tony and Smith, Chris, 1994, *Global Japanization? The Transnational Transformation of the Labour Process*, London: Routledge.

Fan, Ying, 1998, *The Transfer of Western Management to China*, Management Learning.

Fang, Tony, 2006, Negotiation: The Chinese style, *Journal of Business and Industrial Marketing*, 21(1), 50–60.

Farh, Jiing-Lih, Cannella, Albert A., and Lee, Cynthia, 2006, Approaches to scale development in chinese management research, *Management and Organisation Review*, 2(3), 301–318.

Fenby, Jonathan, 2016, *Will China Dominate the 21st Century?* Cambridge: Polity Press.

Ferner, Anthony, 1997, Country of origin effects and HRM in multinational companies, *Human Resource Management Journal*, 7(1), 19–37.

Ferner, Anthony and Quintanilla, Javier, 1998, Multinationals, national business systems and HRM: The enduring influence of national identity or a process of 'Anglo-Saxionisation', *International Journal of Human Resource Management*, 94(4), 710–731.

Fewsmith, Joseph, 2010, *China Today, Tomorrow*, Margland: Rowman & Littlefield, p. 189.

Fisman, Raymond, 2001, Estimating the value of political connections, *American Economic Review*, 91, 1095–1102.

Fitzgerald, Stephen, 2015, *Comrade Ambassador*, Melbourne: Melbourne University Press.

Friedberg, Aaron L., 2011, *A Contest for Supremacy: China, America and the Struggle for Mastery in Asia*, New York: W.W. Norton.

Fuller, Douglas, 2016, *Paper Tigers, Hidden Dragons: Firms and the Political Economy of China's Technological Development*, Oxford: Oxford University Press.

Gallo, Frank T., 2011, *Business Leadership in China: How to Blend Western Practices with Chinese Wisdom*, New York: John Wiley & Sons.

Gamble, Jos and Huang, Qihai, 2009, The transfer of organisational practice: A diachronic perspective from China, *International Journal of Human Resource Management*, 20, 1683–1703.

Gamer, Robert E. 2012, *Understanding Contemporary China*, 4th edn., Boulder: Lynne Rienner Publishers.

Ghauri, Pervez and Fang, Tony, 2001, Negotiating with the Chinese: A Socio-cultural analysis, *Journal of World Business*, 36(3), 303–325.

Gill, Bates and Jakobson, Linda, 2017, *China Matters — Getting It Right for Australia*, Bundoora: La Trobe University Press.

Graham, John L. and Lam, N. Mark, 2003, The Chinese negotiation, *Harvard Business Review*, 81(10), 82–91.

Groves, Theodore, Hong, Yongmiao, McMillan, James, and Naughton, Barry, 1995, China's evolving managerial labour market, *Journal of Political Economy*, 103(4), 873–892.

Gulati, Ranjay, Nohria, Nitin, and Zaheer, Akar, 2000, Strategic networks, *Strategic Management Journal*, 21, 203–215.

Haft, Jeremy R., 2015, *Unmade in Chain — The Hidden Truth About China's Economic Miracle*, Cambridge, Polity Press.

Hall, Edward T., 1976, *Beyond Culture*, New York: Anchor Books.

Halper, Stefan, 2010, *The Beijing Consensus: How China's Authoritarian Model Will Dominate the Twenty-First Century*, New York: Basic Books.

Hamel, Gary and Prahalad, C.K., 1996, *Competing for the Future*, Boston: Harvard Business Review Press.

Hambrick, Donald C. and Mason, Phyllis M., 1984, Upper echelons: The organisation as a reflection of its top managers, *Academy of Management Review*, 9, 193–206.

Hang, Haimig, 2013, International management education in China: A blessing to a curse? in Tsang, D., Kazeroony, H.H., and Ellis, G. (eds.), *The Routledge Companion to International Management Education*, New York: Routledge.

Hill, Charles W.L., 2011, *International Management — Competing in the Global Marketplace*, New York: McGraw-Hill.

Hoffman, John W. and Enright, Michael, J. (eds.), 2008, *China into the Future: Making Sense of the World's Most Dynamic Economy*, Singapore: John Wiley & Sons (Singapore).

Hofstede, Geert, 1984, Culture's consequences: International differences in work-related values, *Administrative Science Quarterly*, 38(1), 132–134.

Hofstede, Geert, 1993, Cultural constraints in management theories, academy of management executive. 7.1, February, 81–94.

Hofstede, Geert and Usunier, Jean-claude, 1996, Hofstede's dimensions of culture and their influence on international business negotiations, in Ghauri, P. and Usunier, J., (eds.), *International Business Negotiations*, Oxford: Pergamon, pp. 119–129.

Hofstede, Geert, 2001, *Culture's Consequences: Comparing Values, Behaviours, Institutions and Organisations across Nations*, 2nd edn., Thousand Oaks, CA: Sage Publishers.

Hofstede, Geert, 2005, *Culture and Organisations: Software of the Mind*, New York: McGraw-Hill.

Hout, Thomas and Michael, David, 2014, *A Chinese Approach to Management*, Boston: Harvard Business Review.

Huczynski, Andrzey, 1996, *Influencing within Organizations*, Upper Saddle River, Prentice Hall.

Hymer, Stephen, 1976, *The International Operations of National Firms: A Study of Direct Investment*, Cambridge: MIT Press.

Jacques, Martin, 2009, *When China Rules the World*, New York: Penguin Books.

Johnson, Gerry and Scholes, Kevan, 2008, *Exploring Corporate Strategy*, 8th edn., London: FT Prentice Hall.

Julian, Craig C., Ahmed, Zafar U., and Xu, Junqian (eds.), 2014, *Research Handbook on the Globalization of Chinese Firms*, London: Edward Elgar.

Kaynak, Erdener, 2001, *Management Education in a Chinese Setting*, London: Routledge.

Kennedy, Scott, '*Made in China 2025*', Centre for Strategic and International Studies, 2015, https://csis.org/publication/made-china-2025.

Kluckhohn, Florence R. and Strodtbeck, Fred L., 1961, *Variations in Value Orientations*. New York: Peterson.

Khurana, Rakesh and Nohria, Nitin, 2008, *It's Time to Make Management a True Profession*, Boston: Harvard Business Review.

Kissinger, Henry, 2011, *On China*, New York: Penguin Press.

Kissinger, Henry, 2014, *World Order*, London: Allen Lane.

Kling, Gerhard and Weitzel, Utz, 2011, The internationalization of Chinese companies: Firm characteristics, industry effects and corporate governance, *Research in International Business and Finance*, 25(3), 357–372.

Kobb, Joshua, 2007, *Management Education in China*, www.iedp.com/Management_Education_in_China, 24 May, 2015.

KPMG/University of Sydney, 2014, *Demystifying Chinese Investment in Australia: Chinese Investors in Australia Survey 2014*, www.kpmg.com.au.

Koller, Tim, Goedhart, Marc and Wessels, David, 2015, *Valuation: Measuring and Managing the Value of Companies*, 6th edn., New York: John Wiley & Sons.

Lamb, Peter and Currie, Graeme, 2012, Eclipsing adaptation: The translation of the US MBA model in China, *Management Learning*, 43, 217–230.

Landes, David, S., 1998, *The Wealth and Poverty of Nations*, London: Little, Brown, p. 342.

Larcon, Paul, 2008, *Chinese Multinationals*, Singapore: World Scientific Publishing.

Lardy, Nicholas R., 2014, *Markets over Mao Zedong: The Rise of Private Business in China*, Washington D.C. PIIE Press.

Lau, Agnes and Roffey, Bet, 2002, *Management Education and Development in China: A Research Note*, Australian National University, http://ncdsnet. anu.edu.au, 12 June, 2015.

Li, Mingfang, Wong, Yim-Yu and Wang, Qun, 2005, Management education in the Greater China economy: Challenges and Task, in Alon, Ilan and McIntyre, John R. (eds.), 2005, *Business and Management Education in China: Transition, Pedagogy and Training*, Singapore: World Scientific Pub Co., pp. 3–18.

Li, Hongbin, Meng, Lingsheng, Wang, Qian, and Zhou, Li-An, 2008, Political connections, financing and firm performance: Evidence from Chinese private firms, *Journal of Development Economics*, 87, 283–299.

Littrell, Romie F., 2005, Teaching Students from confucian cultures, in Alon, Ilan and McIntyre, John R. (eds.), *Business and Management Education in China: Transition, Pedagogy and Training*, Singapore: World Scientific Pub Co., pp. 115–135.

Liu, Shimin, 2006, Developing China's future managers: Learning from the West, *Education & Training*, 48(1), 6–14.

Lou, Yadong, 2002, Partnering with foreign firms: How do Chinese managers view the governance and importance of contracts? *Asia Pacific Journal of Management*, 19, 127–151.

Lu, Y., and Heard, Rachel, 1995, Socialised economic action: A comparison of strategic investment decision-making in China and Britain, *Organisational Studies*, 16, 395–424.

Maddison, Angus, 2006, *The World Economy: A Millennial Perspective*, OECD, Paris — see also Kissinger, Henry, 2011, *On China*, New York: Penguin Press, p. 12.

Martin, Roger and Golsby-Smith, Tony, Management is much more than a Science, *Harvard Business Review*, September–October 2017, pp. 129–135.

McGregor, Richard, 2012, *The Party: The Secret World of China's Communist Rulers*, New York: Harper Perennial.

McKinnon, Ronald, 1973, *Money & Capital in Economic Development*, Washington D.C.: Brooklyn Institution.

McKinsey & Co. (2017), *Making Sense of Chinese Outbound M&A*, July, 2017.

McKinsey & Co, (2016). *What Next for China's Booming Fintech Sector?* July.

McSweeney, Brendan, 2002, Hofstede's model of national cultural differences and their consequences: A triumph of faith — a failure of analysis, *Human Relations*, 55(1), 89–118.

Mead, Richard, and Andrews, Tim G., 2009, *International Management*, New York: John Wiley & Sons.

Meister, Jeanne, 1998, *Corporate Universities: Lessons in Building a World-class Work Force*, New York: McGraw-Hill.

Micklethwait, John and Wooldridge, Adrian, 2014, *The Fourth Revolution — The Global Race to Reinvent the State*, London: Penguin Books.

Midler, Paul, 2011, *Poorly Made in China: An Insider's Account of the China Production Game*, Hoboken: Wiley.

Miles, Michael, 2003, Negotiating with the Chinese: Lessons from the field, *The Journal of Applied Behavioural Science*, 39(4), 453–472.

Miles, Lilian, 2006, The application of Anglo-Saxon corporate practices in societies influenced by confucian values, *Business and Society Review*, 111(3), 305–321.

Mintzberg, Henry, 2004, *Managers Not MBAs*, San Francisco: BK Publishers.

Mufl, Katrin and Dyllick, Thomas, 2013, *Management Education for the World: A Vision for Business Schools Serving People and Planet*, Cheltenham Edward Elgar Publishers.

Nachum, Lilac, 2010, When is foreignness an asset or liability? Explaining the performance differential between foreign and local firms, *Journal of Management*, 36(3), 714–739.

Naughton, Barry, 2006, *The Chinese Economy: Growth and Transition*, Cambridge, Mass.; MIT Press.

Naughton, Barry, 2010, Economic growth: From high-speed to high-quality, in Fewsmith, Joseph (ed.), *China Today, China Tomorrow*, Lanham: Rowman & Littlefield Publishers, Inc.

Nee, Victor and Opper, Sonja, 2012, *Capitalism from Below*, Harvard: Harvard University Press.

Newman, Karen L., and Nollen, Stanley D. 1996, Culture and congruence: The fit between management practices and national culture, *Journal of International Business Studies*, 27(4), 753–779.

Newell, Sue, 1999, The transfer of management knowledge to China: Building learning communities rather than translating Western textbooks? *Education + Training*, 41(6/7), 286–294.

Nolan, Peter, Jin Zhang, and Chunhang Liu, 2007, *Implications for Firm-Level Catch-up and Developing Economies, The Global Business Revolution and the Cascade Effect*, Basingstoke UK: Palgrave Macmillan.

Nolan, Peter, 2012, *Is China Buying the World?* London: Polity.

Nolan, Peter, 2014, *Chinese Firms, Global Firms — Industrial Policy in the Era of Globalisation*, London: Routledge.

Nye, Joseph S., 2004, *Soft Power: The Means of Success in World Politics*, New York: Public Affairs Press.

OECD, 2005, *Improving the Productivity of the Business Sector*, Economic Surveys: China, Chapter 2, Paris: Organisation for Economic Cooperation and Development.

OECD, 2012, *Glossary of Foreign Direct Investment Terms and Definition*, p. 7.

O'Connor, Neale G., 2005, *Management Control of Multinational Enterprises in China*, Singapore: McGraw-Hill Education (Asia).

Park, Seung Ho and Luo, Yadong, 2001, Guanxi and organisational dynamics: Organisational networking in Chinese firms, *Strategic Management Journal*, 22, 455–477.

Paulson, Henry, M. Jr, 2015, *Dealing With China*, New York: Twelve.

Pei, Minxin, 2006, *China's Trapped Transition: The Limits of Development Autocracy*, Boston: Harvard University Press.

Pei, Minxin, 2016, *China's Crony Capitalism: The Dynamics of Regime Decay*, Boston: Harvard University Press.

Peng, Mike W. and Luo, Yadong, 2000, Managerial ties and firm performance in a transition economy: The nature of a micro-macro link, *Academy of Management Journal*, 43(3), 486–501.

Peteraf, M.A., 1993, The cornerstones of competitive advantage: A resource-based view, *Strategic Management Journal*, 14(3), 179–191.

Peyrefitte, Alain, 1993, *The Collision of Two Civilisations: The British Expedition to China* 1792–1794, London: Harvill, Harper Collins.

Porter, Michael E., 1980, *Competitive Strategy*, New York: Free Press.

Porter, Michael E., 1990, *The Competitive Advantage of Nations*. New York: Free Press.

Porter, Michael E., 1998, *Determinants of National Competitive Advantage: Competitive Advantage*, New York: Free Press.

Porter, Lyman W. and McKibbin, Lawrence E., 1988, *Management Education and Development: Drift or Thrust into the 21st Century*, London: McGraw-Hill.

Prahalad, Coimbatore K. and Hamel, Gary, 1990, *The Core Competence of the Corporation*, Boston: Harvard Business Review, May–June.

Pye, Lucian W., 1982, *Chinese Commercial Negotiating Style*, Cambridge, MA: Oelgeschlager, Gun & Hain.

Pye, Lucian W., 1986, The China trade: Making the deal, *Harvard Business Review*, 64(4), 74–80.

Reilly, James, 2013, *China's Economic Statecraft: Turning Wealth into Power*, Lowy Institute for International Policy, November, www.lowyinstitue.org.

Rosch, Jan-Frederik, 2013, *Internationalisation of Chinese Multinational Corporations: Qualitative Evidence from Western Europe*, Amsterdam: European Management Publication.

Rosenzweig, Philip and Nohria, Nitin, 1994, Influences on human resource management practices in multinational corporations, *Journal of International Business Studies*, 25(2), 229–251.

Rugman, Alan M., and Li, Jing, 2007, Will China's Multinational Succeed Globally or Regionally? *European Management Journal*, 5, 333–343.

Rugman, Alan M., 2010, Globalization of Chinese enterprises, *International Trade Journal*, 24, 352–354.

Sadun, Raffaella, Bloom, Nicholas, and Van Reenen, John, 2017, Why do we undervalue competent management? *Harvard Business Review*, September–October, pp. 121–127.

Said, Edward, 1976, *Arabs, Islam and the Dogmas of the West*, reproduced in Macfie, A., 2000, *Orientalism: A Reader*, Edinburgh: Edinburgh University Press, pp. 104–105.

Said, Edward, 1978, *Orientalism*, New York, Vintage Books.

Scarborough, Jack, 1998, Comparing Chinese and Western cultural roots, *Business Horizons*, 41(6), 15–24.

Sen, Amartya, 1999, *Development as Freedom*, New York: Alfred A. Knopf.

Shaw, Edward S., 1973, *Financial Deepening in Economic Development*, Oxford: Oxford University Press.

Schmidt, Tobias and Sofka, Wolfgang, 2009, Liability of foreignness as a barrier to knowledge spillovers: Lost in translation? *Journal of International Marketing*, 15(4), 460–474.

Schoemaker, Paul J.H., 2008, The future challenges of business: Rethinking management education and research, *California Management Review*, 50(3), 119–139.

Shambaugh, David, 2012, Are China's multinational corporations really multinational? *East Asia Quarterly*, IV(II), 7.

Shambaugh, David, 2016, *China's Future?* Cambridge: Polity Press.

Shiller, Robert J., 2000, *Irrational Exuberance*, Princeton: Princeton University Press.

Shirk, Susan L., 2007, *China Fragile Superpower*, Oxford: Oxford University Press.

Smith, Adam, (1776, 1976), *An Inquiry into the Nature and Cause of the Wealth of Nations*, Chicago: University of Chicago Press.

Snow, Edgar 1971, A Conversation with Mao Zedong, *LIFE*, 70(16), April 30.

Solinger, Dorothy J., 1998, *China's Floating Population: Implications for State and Society*, in Goldman, Merle, and MacFarquhar, Roderick (eds.), *The Paradox of China's Post-Mao Reforms*, Boston: Harvard University Press.

Solinger, Dorothy J., 2001, Why we cannot count the "unemployed," *The China Quarterly*, 167, 671–688.

Solow, Robert, 2000, *Growth Theory*, 2nd edn., New York: Oxford University Press.

Song, Ligang, 2001, Institutional change, trade composition and export supply potential in China, in Garnaut, Ross and Huang, Yiping (eds.), *Growth without Miracles: Readings on the Chinese Economy in the Era of Reform*, Oxford: Oxford University Press.

Song, James Y., 2005, Business ethics in China: Current understanding and a mechanistic model of cultural evolution in Alon, Ilan and McIntyre, John R. (eds.), 2005, *Business and Management Education in China: Transition, Pedagogy and Training*, Singapore: World Scientific Pub Co., pp. 67–88.

Southworth, David B., 1999, Building a business school in China: The case of the China Europe International Business School (CEIBS), *Education + Training*, 41(6/7), 325–331.

Starkey, Ken and Tiratsoo, Nick, 2007, *The Business School and the Bottom Line*, New York: Cambridge University Press.

Stiglitz, Joseph E. and Weiss, Andrew, 1981, Credit rationing in markets with imperfect information, *American Economic Review*, 71, 393–410.

Stiglitz, Joseph E., 1985, Credit markets and the control of capital, *Journal of Money, Credit and Banking*, 17(2), 133–152.

Strauss, Anselm L., 1987, *Qualitative Analysis for Social Scientists*, Cambridge, Cambridge University Press.

Strauss, Anselm L. and Corbin, Juliet, 1990, *Basics of Qualitative Research: Grounded Theory and Techniques*, Thousand Oaks: Sage.

Srinivasan, Bhu, 2017, *Americana: A 400-Year History of American Capitalism*, London: Penguin Press.

Tang, Jie and Ward, Anthony, 2003, *The Changing Face of Chinese Management*, London: Routledge.

Taleb, Nassim Nicholas, 2007, *Black Swan: The Impact of the Highly Probable*, New York: Random House.

Thaler, Richard H. and Sunstein, Cass R., 2008, *Nudge*, London: Penguin Books.

Tian, Xiaowen, 2007, *Managing International Business in China*, New York: Cambridge University Press.

Thomas, Jesu R., 2014, *History of Management Education*, Anil Pinto, www.anilpinto.blogspot.com/2014/history-of-managment.

Thomas, Howard, Lorange, Peter, and Sheth, Jagdish, 2013, *The Business School in the Twenty First Century,* New York: Cambridge University Press.

Torrens, Chris, 2010, Doing Business in China, *The Economist,* London: Profile Books.

Tse, Edward, 2015, *China's Disruptors,* London: Portfolio Penguins.

Tselichtchev, Ivan, 2012, *China Versus the West: The Global Power Shift of the 21st Century,* Singapore, Wiley & Co.

Tsui, Anne and Lau, Chung Ming, 2002, *The Management of Enterprises in the People's Republic of China,* Berlin: Springer Publishers.

Tsui, Anne S., 2006, Contextualisation in Chinese management research, *Management and Organisation Review,* 2, 1–13.

Tuong Anh, Nguyen Thi, and Hing, Doan Quang, 2016, *Chinese Outward Foreign Direct Investment: Is ASEAN a New Destination?* World Trade Institute, Working Paper No. 06/2016 www.wti.org.

Van de Berg, H., 2002, *International Trade and Economic Growth,* in Van den Berg, H. (ed.), *International Economics A Heterodox Approach,* Chapter 5, New York: McGraw-Hill/Irwin.

Venkatesan, Ravi, 2013, *Conquering the Chaos,* New York: Harvard Business Review Press.

Vogel, Ezra, F., 2011, *Deng Xiaoping and the Transformation of China,* Boston: Harvard University Press.

Wang, Xiaoyun, He, Wei, and Yu, Kaicheng, 2005, *East Meets West: The Dilemma of Management Pedagogy in China* in Alon, Ilan and McIntyre, John R., (eds.), *Business and Management Education in China: Transition, Pedagogy and Training,* Singapore: World Scientific Pub Co.

Wang, Chengai. *et al.,* 2011, *What Drives Outward FDI of Chinese Firms?* Boston: International Business Review.

Wagner, Tony, 2012, *Creating Innovators: The Making of Young People who will Change the World,* New York: Scribner Publishers.

Warner, Malcolm, 1991, *Management Education and Training Strategies in the People's Republic of China: An Overview,* Research Paper No.1991/8, Management Studies Group, Cambridge University, Cambridge.

Warner, Malcolm and Goodhall, Keith (eds.), 2009, *Management Training and Development in China: Educating Managers in a Globalised Economy,* London: Routledge.

Warner, Malcolm, 2014, *Understanding Management in China — Past, Present and Future,* London: Routledge.

Welch, Jack, 2005, *Winning,* New York: Harper Collins.

Wen, Xiao and Liyun, Liu, 2015, *Internationalisation of China's Privately-Owned Enterprises*, Beijing: World Scientific, Zhenjiang University Press.

Westad, Odd Arne, 2012, *Restless Empire — China and the World since 1750*, New York: Basic Books.

Williamson, Peter, Ramamurti, Ravi, Fleury, Afonso, and Fleury, Maria Tereza, 2013, *The Competitive Advantage of Emerging Market Multinationals*, Cambridge: Cambridge University Press.

Williamson, Peter and Yin, Eden, 2014, Accelerated Innovation: The New Challenge from China, *MIT Sloan Management Review*, Summer.

Winchester, Simon, 2008, *Bomb, Book and Compass — Joseph Needham and the Great Secrets of China*, London: Penguin Books.

Womack, James P., Jones, Daniel T., and Roos, Daniel, 1990, *The Machine that Changed the World*, New York: Free Press.

Xi Jinping, 2014, *The Governance of China*, Beijing: Foreign Language Press.

Xin, Katherine and Haijie, Wang, 2011, *Culture Clash in the Boardroom*, Boston: Harvard Business Review.

Xin, Katherine R. and Pearce, Jone L., 1996, Guanxi: Connections as substitutes for formal institutional support, *Academy of Management Journals*, 39, 1641–1658.

Yang, Hailan and Morgan, Stephen L., 2011, *Business Strategy and Corporate Governance in the Chinese Consumer Electronics Sector*, Oxford: Chandos Pub.

Yeung, Anthony and Xinpeng, Katherine, 2011, *The Globalisation of Chinese Companies: Strategies for Conquering International Markets*, New York: John Wiley & Sons.

Yip, George and McKern, Bruce, 2016, *China's Next Strategic Advantage: From Imitation to Innovation*, Boston: MIT Press.

Yuan, Lin, and Pangarkar, Nitin, 2010, Inertia versus mimicry in location choices by Chinese multinationals, *International Marketing Review*, 27(3), 295–315.

Zang, Xiaowei, 2011, *Understanding Chinese Society*, New York: Routledge.

Zhang, Xiaohe, 2000, Motivation, objectives, locations and partner selections of foreign invested enterprises in China, *Journal of the Asia-Pacific Economy*, 5(3), 190–203.

Zhang, Weiwei, 2011, *The China Wave — Rise of a Civilization State*, Shanghai: World Century.

Zhang, Wenxian and Wang, Huiyao (eds.), 2011, *Entrepreneurial and Business Elites of China: The Chinese Returnees Who Have Shaped Modern China*, New York: Emerald Group Publishing.

Zhao Ziyang, 2009, *Prisoner of the State — The Secret Journal of Chinese Premier Zhao Ziyang*, London: Pocket Books.

Zhun, Jinqi and Wei, William, 2014, HR strategy and practice in Chinese multinational companies in Julian, Craig C., Ahmed, Zafar U., and Xu, Junqian (eds.), *Research Handbook on the Globalization of Chinese Firms*, Edward Elgar, UK, pp. 162–188.

Index

Printed in the United States
By Bookmasters